Praise for *What's in It*

"In a world where loneliness and disconn[...]
Joe Polish steps up with crystal clear, timele[...]
relationships that benefit you and the world. These lessons come from a
modern master of networking with real, deep friendships. Read this book
to help the world be a better place."

— **Dave Asprey**, founder of Bulletproof Coffee and four-time
New York Times best-selling author

"Joe Polish outlines the game plan for success and peace of mind that anyone
can adopt via the radical concept of generosity. He shows you how to make the
world a better place and become wealthy without sacrificing your soul."

— **Chris Voss**, former FBI hostage negotiator, CEO and founder of
The Black Swan Group, and author of *Never Split the Difference*

"I'm always irritated by how-to books written by people who've never
proved they know how to. Joe Polish's What's in It for Them? *is exactly*
the opposite. . . . He is an absolute master at establishing relationships with
people he's in business with. . . . This indeed is the critical element, above
and beyond having a great product and knowing how to market it, that
turns entrepreneurship into success. And makes it fun!"

— **Steven Pressfield**, best-selling author of *The War of Art* and *Turning Pro*

"One of Joe's greatest gifts is connection: his uncanny ability to connect
us with new ideas, new possibilities, new people, and most importantly,
ourselves. This book is a treasure, filled with profound wisdom and practical
strategies that will benefit you and those you serve for years to come."

— **Marie Forleo**, #1 *New York Times* best-selling author of
Everything Is Figureoutable

*"*What's in It for Them? *brilliantly modernizes relationship mastery with*
an entertaining, uplifting, and very raw honesty that is often lost as authors
try to write something that will offend no one and have a little something for
everyone. Joe's book provides priceless, actionable, step-by-step strategies that
you can start using right away to build better relationships, live a better life,
and create positive change and impact in the world."

— **Roland Frasier**, co-founder and/or principal of five different
Inc. Magazine fastest-growing companies

"Everyone knows people prefer to do business within strong relationships. The
unanswered question was always exactly how to build those relationships.
Not anymore. This brilliant book shows us precisely when and how to do it.
That's what makes it brilliant . . . and indispensable."

— **Robert B. Cialdini**, author of *Influence* and *Pre-Suasion*

WHAT'S IN IT FOR THEM?

ALSO BY JOE POLISH

9 Genius Networking Principles
to Get What You Want by Helping
Others Get What They Want

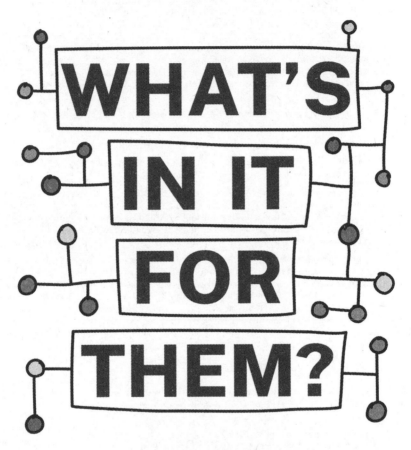

WHAT'S
IN IT
FOR
THEM?

JOE POLISH

BUSINESS

HAY HOUSE, INC.
Carlsbad, California • New York City
London • Sydney • New Delhi

Published in the United States by: Hay House, Inc.: www.hayhouse.com®
Published in Australia by: Hay House Australia Pty. Ltd.: www.hayhouse.com.au
Published in the United Kingdom by: Hay House UK, Ltd.: www.hayhouse.co.uk
Published in India by: Hay House Publishers India: www.hayhouse.co.in

*Cover design: the*BookDesigners • *Cover illustrations:* Gapingvoid
Interior design: Alex Head/Draft Lab • *Indexer:* J S Editorial, LLC

**Cataloging-in-Publication Data is on file
at the Library of Congress**

Tradepaper ISBN: 978-1-4019-7585-2
E-book ISBN: 978-1-4019-6011-7
Audiobook ISBN: 978-1-4019-6029-2

10 9 8 7 6 5 4 3 2 1
1st edition, November 2022
2nd edition, October 2023

Printed in the United States of America

This product uses paper and materials from responsibly sourced forests. For more information, please go to: bookchainproject.com/home.

To Sean Stephenson, Dave Kekich, and Dr. Janice Dorn, three incredible humans and dear friends who contributed so much to the world; to my chief of staff, Eunice Miller, who has been with me for over 27 years; and to all my team members at Piranha Marketing and Genius Network.

A portion of the proceeds from the sale of *What's in It for Them?* will be donated to Genius Recovery, a nonprofit organization created by Joe Polish to change the global conversation around addiction and recovery. **www.GeniusRecovery.org**

CONTENTS

Introduction..xv

Chapter 1: How Are They Suffering and How Can I Help?......1

Chapter 2: Invest Time, Attention, Money, Effort, and
Energy in Relationships.......................33

Chapter 3: Be the Person They Always Answer the
Phone For......................................59

Chapter 4: Be Useful, Grateful, and Valuable................87

Chapter 5: Treat Others as ~~You~~ They Love to Be Treated.....111

Chapter 6: Avoid Formalities and Be Fun and
Memorable (Not Boring).......................137

Chapter 7: Appreciate People............................157

Chapter 8: Give Value on the Spot.........................181

Chapter 9: Get as Close to In-Person as You Can...........207

Conclusion..229
Lessons from Joe's Sabbatical................................234
Resources..235
Index..237
Acknowledgments...249
About the Author...254

We have set up a simple way for you to access
the resources, tools, and exercises you'll
find throughout this book. Just point your
smartphone at the QR code below and it
will take you directly to the resources page:
www.WIIFTbook.com/resources

INTRODUCTION

I'm going to start by giving you the 30,000-foot view of this book on page one:

The secret to success in life and in business is learning how to connect and form relationships with other people—*and most people don't know how to do that.*

If you've ever heard entrepreneurs say they hate "networking" (or if you've been one of the entrepreneurs saying it), it's usually for that very reason: they don't know the right way to do it. "Networking" has come to mean shallow conversations, transactional relationships, and the anxiety of impressing other people so that they'll do something for you. But that's not what networking has to be—and that's what you'll discover in the pages ahead.

The book you're holding wouldn't even exist if Dale Carnegie hadn't written his classic *How to Win Friends and Influence People*. I love that book, and it remains essential reading to this day. But as I've grown as an entrepreneur over the last 30-plus years, I've realized it needs a significant update. I've learned firsthand (sometimes the hard way) that your success and happiness don't depend on simply winning friends and influencing people. They depend on winning the *right* friends and influencing the *right* people—and identifying who those people are in the first place. The more successful you become in life, the more important these skills become.

I've actually created a framework for filtering right-fit people from wrong-fit ones. Any relationship that's "ELF" (Easy, Lucrative & Fun) is the right fit, and any relationship that's "HALF" (Hard, Annoying, Lame & Frustrating) is the wrong fit. You can have ELF clients and ELF team members, or you can have HALF clients and HALF team members. In the past, I was willing to deal with HALFs because those connections have led to lucrative opportunities. It takes courage to walk away from those connections. But at this point in my life, I'm committed to having only ELF relationships.

That's what I want for you, and that is the purpose of this book: to change your perspective on how you interact with others so you can make the *right* connections with the *right* people in the *right* way, in any situation.

To do this masterfully, the key is to start by asking one simple question:

What's in it for them?

By asking this question, you shift the focus off you and onto the ways you can be useful to others. You get out of the transactional networking mindset and start to form transformational, meaningful, and collaborative relationships (which are usually ELF, by the way).

Asking this question over and over lets you connect with people by figuring out what they need, helping them get it, and making their lives better. In a very real way, by asking this question, you're reducing other people's suffering. By reducing others' suffering, you become a magnetic and valuable person whom people value and want to collaborate with. And through the rich relationships you form in this way and the doors these relationships open, you reduce your *own* suffering, improve your own life, and make the world a better place.

But before we get into that, you may be wondering: Who am I to talk about all this?

I'm Joe Polish (pronounced like shoe polish, not like the nationality). I have been a troubled kid, an active addict, a recovery advocate, a professional marketer, and so much more. Today, I'm the owner of a 40-acre ghost town in Cleator, Arizona, and co-founder of a virtual reality company, GeniusX, but I'm probably most known for founding two of the highest-level marketing groups in the world, Genius Network and 100K, for which members pay an annual membership fee of $25,000 and $100,000 respectively—the original "mastermind" model that has been adopted by countless others over the years. I've been called "the most connected man on the planet." *(I wouldn't describe myself that way, but it's what others have said.)* My mission today is twofold: to build a better entrepreneur by teaching people how to have an ELF life and business, and to change the global conversation about how others view and treat addicts. These may sound different, but to me, they're deeply intertwined.

That's where I am today, but it's not where I started.

I started my working life as a dead-broke carpet cleaner in Chandler, Arizona.

I started my own carpet-cleaning business with all my savings—$1,500—because I wanted a better future and I didn't have any better options. I quickly learned that carpet cleaning is dirty, hard work. Over time, I moved away from doing the actual cleaning, shifted my business toward selling carpet-cleaning services, and eventually

moved into selling and marketing products and services—
billions of dollars' worth—for businesses of all kinds.

As my business grew, there were moments, lessons,
and relationships that helped propel me forward. I think
of these as "dominoes," because like dominoes falling,
each experience leads to the next one, in a chain reaction
that keeps going and going.

You never know how far one domino can take you.
And I hope this book becomes a domino in *your* life, the
one that finally falls and begins a cascade of change and
success for you.

Here's how the book works:

- Each chapter explores a core principle of connection based on the Magic Rapport Formula,
  originally coined by Fabienne Fredrickson,
  which I've spoken about extensively on my
  I Love Marketing podcast with my co-host
  Dean Jackson.

- Each chapter shares stories from my work with
  Genius Network members and from my personal life. You'll spot some names you'll probably recognize. They're here because I know
  these people, have worked with them, and
  have learned a lot from them.

- Each chapter highlights key takeaways, or
  "dominoes," throughout, with questions to
  help you reflect on how the principles play out
  in your own life.

- Alongside the positive aspects of each principle, each chapter also points out the downsides and potential pitfalls that can come with
  embracing them—so you can steer clear.

- Each chapter ends with specific exercises and action steps I've used to coach some of the world's most successful entrepreneurs in Genius Network. Some of them may seem completely out of your comfort zone—or even out of left field—so much so that some people won't ever try them. I know that. But if you do, the results will be huge. (You can thank me later.)

Before we begin, I want to offer a couple of disclaimers. First, though a lot of this book talks about the value of being kind in interactions with others, you can often interpret "kind" in a variety of ways—meaning cool, interesting, engaging, even sarcastic, depending on the context. The point is to deal with people at a level they can understand and respond to.

Second, for all the advice in this book, I don't claim to offer "the" answers for specific issues. For best results, approach what you read here with the same attitude as a line they often say in 12-step rooms: "Take what you like and leave the rest."

What's important to realize is that this book is not just about capabilities. It's also about character—your own and others'—and understanding how character creates the kinds of connections that can change your life. So while I'm going to give you a wealth of practical tools and specific strategies for success, I'm also going to ask you to delve pretty deep into some psychological and emotional territory along the way.

I've been doing a lot of that myself lately. As I wrote these pages, I had just finished a year-long sabbatical to reassess and reflect on how much my life, business, and relationships have grown over the years. I've sought to better understand how I can be useful to the right people, so I can better share this knowledge with you.

I started my career asking, *"What's in it for them?"*

Years later, I still ask the same question, though some of my answers have changed. My hope is that this book inspires you to start asking the same thing.

A NOTE TO THE READER

In my experience, people who are interested in personal development read a lot of books. They are always looking for new ideas and concepts to take them and their performance to the next level. This book is for those people, but it's also a little different.

Everything I wrote in this book, I wrote with the assumption that the readers picking it up would be truly conscientious people who care about helping others and being more effective givers in the world.

In that spirit, I ask that you truly take your time with these pages and not treat these ideas as gimmicks or bonuses on top of something else. My hope is that you will treat these ideas as foundational.

If you internalize these principles and integrate them in your life, you will become so much more effective at relationships, learning, and interacting with people in almost every way.

If you truly absorb the ideas in this book, they will help you get so much more out of every other book, seminar, course, and self-improvement endeavor you'll ever pursue.

They will enhance everything you do in life for one simple reason: everything you do in life involves other people.

HOW ARE THEY SUFFERING AND HOW CAN I HELP?

I don't remember my childhood all that well, but I have three memories that really stand out.

The first is when I was four years old and jumping on a bed. Almost violently my father yanked me off the bed. We were in a weird little house in Kerrville, Texas, that had my father's locksmith shop in the front and our living area in the back. My mom was lying in the bed, and I think she wanted me there, but my father may have thought I was hurting her. She had ovarian cancer, but I didn't know that. I just wanted to have fun with my mom.

My second memory is huddling with my brother and father around my mother's hospital bed. She had tubes up her nose and told us something along the lines of "Listen to your father. Love the Lord. Be good. I love you." That was the last time I saw her.

My third memory is seeing my father leaning against a tree and sobbing. It's a surreal moment because I don't recall where we were or who else was there. All I remember is his massive pain, me trying to comfort him, and feeling totally lost.

Now that I'm an adult, I know there's no telling how people will choose to react to situations. The way I reacted to my mom's death and my father's suffering was simple: I just wanted to take away my father's pain however I could. More than that, I wanted to comfort those around me.

For example, a tree behind our building was scheduled to be torn down to make way for new construction. I thought the animals that lived in that tree would die. So when the site was empty, I marched out to the bulldozer parked there and tried to form a plan. Perhaps if I blocked the wheels, the bulldozer couldn't move. If the machine couldn't move, the tree couldn't be torn down and the animals would live. I ran home and grabbed as many blocks, toys, and empty tin cans as I could carry and packed them under the bulldozer's wheels.

Of course, my plan didn't work. My toys got either run over or returned to me—I can't remember which. The tree came down, but that only made me more determined.

I realized at an early age that the people I loved were suffering, and I unconsciously wanted my life to be about helping people in the most deep and meaningful ways I possibly could. Despite going through my *own* pain and suffering, I chose to do anything I could to add positivity to the world around me. Sometimes I succeeded; sometimes I failed miserably.

But even if I couldn't stop every single bulldozer, I adopted a mindset that has been the foundation of almost all my success. *How are they suffering, and how can I help?*

Domino: To be better at life and relationships, learn to ask, "How are they suffering, and how can I help?"

Question for you: Think about anyone important in your life and ask, "How are they suffering, and how can I help?"

WHAT IS SUFFERING?

Before you can identify and help people who are suffering, you have to know what you're looking for. In brief, *suffering is pain.*

Suffering can be physical, emotional, mental, or spiritual—and you don't have to be religious to be in deep spiritual pain. It encompasses everything from life during wartime to bad weather conditions to physical disabilities. Those obvious kinds of pain are part of the fabric of life that we can all observe, but other types of suffering are harder to see.

There's the emotional suffering of shame, sadness, and regret. The mental anguish of anxiety, paranoia, and depression. The spiritual pain of disconnection, isolation, and addiction.

For a vivid snapshot of spiritual suffering, look at someone in active addiction:

- Physical dependence on drugs and constant discomfort? Check.

- Damaged relationships and warped self-image from out-of-control behavior? Check.

- Compounded mental issues like anxiety, narcissism, and depression? Check.

- Feeling like you're losing your connection to yourself, your loved ones, and the world in general? Check.

In short, there's suffering everywhere, and there's much more than most people realize.

On the physical level, the source of suffering is something anyone can understand. Pain is your hand touching a hot stove and feeling the burn until you take your hand away. Suffering is the gnawing in your stomach when there's not enough food to eat.

But there's also the deeper view of suffering discussed by thinkers like philosopher and author Eckhart Tolle or by the teachings of Zen Buddhism. From that perspective, suffering is not caused merely by a physical experience, but by our thoughts, feelings, beliefs, and judgments about the experience. We multiply our suffering through our attachment to the thoughts and stories we tell ourselves about our experiences and how those stories compound, causing more and more suffering. To quote the author and mystic Neville Goddard, "You never see the outside world, only your own reaction to it." Unless you become purposefully mindful of your reactions and narratives, you will suffer significantly without realizing you are the source.

> **Domino:** Suffering is partially a matter of perspective and of our mindset. In full view of our suffering on any scale, we still have choices: feed the pain or change our perspective.

> **Question for you:** What is the source of your most persistent suffering? Think about something in your life that has frustrated or challenged you for a long time — why is this still causing pain?

IS SUFFERING A BAD THING?

I know what you're thinking: Is he really asking that?

There's no question that suffering is unpleasant. Being in pain increases the chances that we might put others in pain. But what is good or bad depends on your perspective.

But suffering can also create opportunities for connection.

Suffering can be powerful, and it can be useful. The discomfort it brings can help you disconnect from harmful relationships and energy leeches. Or, under different circumstances, suffering can help you connect deeply with other people and form helpful relationships.

Rarely do people stop to consider how relationships are *formed* and what relationships are actually *for*. The relationship is formed for a reason—usually to remove some form of suffering experienced by one of the parties—though the connection transforms both.

Creating quick rapport with people who are suffering is a natural multiplier to success in life, personally and in your career.

My good friend Dan Sullivan, founder of The Strategic Coach® Program, says, "Other people's bad news is your good news." As an entrepreneur, your job is to reduce or remove the challenges others face. You're the good news to another's bad news, the solution to their suffering. You have the key to their compelling and better future.

Connecting with people is about helping them get what they want and helping them reduce or remove what is causing them suffering. I'll repeat what I said in the Introduction: by connecting with others, you reduce your own suffering, improve your own life, have richer relationships, and make the world a better place.

So how exactly do you turn suffering into a tool for connection?

Domino: Suffering can be useful if it creates opportunities for connection.

Question for you: Who could you create deeper connections with by better understanding their suffering?

BECOME A PAIN DETECTIVE

Looking at the memory snippets from when I was four years old, now in my 50s I have a different perspective.

When my dad yanked me off the bed that day, I felt hurt, embarrassed, ashamed, and annoyed. *Me and Mom are in the middle of something here, Dad. Can't you see that?*

My dad clearly *couldn't* see. He didn't understand at that moment that all I wanted to do was spend time with my mom. But at four years old, I didn't really understand my dad either.

Dad grew up dirt poor and felt victimized as the youngest of nine siblings. For a big part of his childhood, he served as a caretaker to the point of codependency. Drafted into the army at a young age, he came out traumatized and even paranoid. After all that, he found happiness with my mom until she died of cancer. Then, once more, he became a solo caretaker.

After my mom died, my father sometimes acted physically, emotionally, and mentally abusive to my brother and me. While he didn't put out cigarettes on our arms, he hit us with belts, shouted, and criticized constantly. Nothing we did was good enough.

Despite how severe he could be, I sensed that my dad *did* love and care and want to provide for us. I felt he did the best he could. Rather than emulating his harsh energy with anger or blame, I chose something else. I chose *curiosity.*

I started to observe closely. Even if my dad walked around with a cloud over his head, I sat in his shop with a huge smile on my face. Customers stopped and commented to my dad, "What a happy kid!"

It wasn't true, of course, but the comment made my dad's mood a little lighter and gave me some breathing room. At some point, something clicked: I observed that my dad was in immense pain—just as much as I was and maybe more. I also observed that just my smile and a few kind words did some pretty heavy lifting. Even without understanding the nuances, that was interesting to me.

As I grew up, I kept smiling, creating space, and offering to help people everywhere I went. I noticed how much power I had to affect others. After my father and brother and I moved from Texas to New Mexico, I started out shy and unpopular in school, but kept practicing my method. I was still being curious about other people. Gradually, I didn't get bullied as much, and I made friends.

My experiments in random kindness seemed to be working. Finding how much pain I could ease in the simplest ways fueled my curiosity more.

How could I turn sadness into joy? Anger into excitement? Suffering into comfort? I was starting to glimpse the energetic field underneath human interactions, the parallel world no one talked about but seemed to rule *everything.*

Domino: Be a pain detective to connect with others. Focus first on the other person and their suffering. You and your possible solutions come second.

Question for you: How has your discernment of people's emotions helped you create connections in the past?

DETERMINE THE EMOTIONAL ATMOSPHERE

My friend and Genius Network member Dr. Don Wood is a former hockey player turned trauma doctor. He didn't grow up with trauma in his life. Having felt safe and secure as a child, he didn't understand why some people had a lot of anxiety and fears. But early in his marriage, his wife had fears from her childhood, and gradually her reactions to things started to make sense to him. He came up with a great term to describe what makes people the way they are: *atmospheric conditions*. "If you understood the atmospheric conditions of everyone's life," he said to me, "it would make sense why they do what they do and why they behave the way they behave."

This important concept is one of the most valuable to understand about connecting with other people: the better you understand their context, the better you can connect with them. It can take some people a lifetime to learn this, but being aware of the concept can accelerate the learning curve.

The atmosphere of my early life turned me into a natural empath, a pain detective, and later in life, a student of other people's atmospheric conditions. It meant getting curious about what turned the gears in their heads. Of course, it also meant figuring out how to make others comfortable, and for me this resulted in pushing down my own needs, having weak boundaries, and getting walked on many times.

But it doesn't have to be that way. And you don't have to be a natural empath to benefit from being a pain detective. By understanding where a person comes from emotionally, you will be able to connect with them.

There are multiple steps to understanding a person's atmospheric conditions, and then utilizing that to make a meaningful connection.

1. Be genuinely curious

Being a pain detective is staying aware of other people's emotions, wanting to learn their stories, and connecting over shared pain. *This is the foundation of learning their emotional atmosphere.* Be *genuinely curious* about other people and willing to help. If you start from that position, so many good things follow.

One big fear people have around connecting with others is knowing what to say. They get stuck in small talk, or feel awkward because they don't know how to listen or how to genuinely be themselves.

That awkwardness is understandable if you think about the emotional place that it's coming from. If you're scrambling for what to say next in a conversation, there's a good chance you're coming from a defensive or avoidant place. Rather than letting the conversation flow and opening your emotions to the other person, you're:

- worried about what you'll say next (or what they'll say)
- afraid there will be pauses in the conversation
- rushing to fill in breaks

In conversations like those, the result is that one person comes off like they're selling themselves to someone else, and it feels inauthentic. It's not "selling" that's the problem, though. The problem is a lack of genuine connection. If the connection is genuine, then "selling" is transformational, not transactional. Remember, it's about them, not about you.

2. Sell yourself authentically

I once asked Dan Sullivan his definition of selling. He said, "Selling is getting someone intellectually engaged in a future result that's good for them and getting them to emotionally commit to take action to achieve that result."

There's an idea out there that selling is manipulative, or even in some sense evil, but by this definition, selling is the most positive behavior in the world. You *are* selling yourself in interactions with people whether you like it or not. If you're not selling your *true* self, you're selling a persona that's a second-rate product you're probably not very good at pitching. The quality of your product comes down to knowing who you are, being honest about that, and focusing on the other person.

When you bring your real self to interactions and present your *real* opinions with kindness, you offer your authentic self to others. In a very real way, you offer them value. By giving them something first before asking for anything in return, you show you're different from other people: You're there to help. You're a giver, first and foremost. Not a taker.

3. Communicate vs. connect vs. escape

There are only three positions any person can have in an interaction where the goal is to bond or connect with others. People are either communicating, connecting, or trying to escape.

If you are truly communicating, you are in an exchange of energy and information. You may not be in perfect sync, but you are passing a ball back and forth. You are exploring each other and learning.

If you are connecting, you've moved beyond communication and you are forming a deeper bond with each other. You recognize yourself to some degree in the other person, creating mutual trust. You have more rapport, comfort, and warmth for the other person.

If you're *not* communicating or connecting, you're trying to escape. You can see this happening on a macro level and also on a micro level as interaction with another ebbs and flows.

How is the other person reacting to what you say?

Are they leaning in or pulling back?

Are they giving short answers or speaking at length?

By knowing about these three positions, you can toggle what you say and how you say it to learn about someone's atmospheric conditions more deeply.

4. Touch the suffering point

Producer Jason Headley made a video called *It's Not about the Nail* that has had more than 20 million views. When you look it up, the video shows a woman complaining about debilitating head pain while a nail protrudes from her forehead. When her partner tries to point out the nail to her, she accuses him of "always trying to fix things" when she just wants him to listen.

There are a few lessons in there, but one is that you have choices when other people present you with their narratives.

First, you can simply empathize and let somebody live in their story. Or, as a pain detective, you can say, "You've got a nail in your head, and we can pull it out."

If a co-worker complains about being overwhelmed but also notes they only had an hour of sleep the night before because their child was sick, a compassionate, empathetic boss who is a pain detective won't just listen to the story. Depending on the employee's reasons for losing sleep, the boss might allow the worker to go home to rest without penalty.

One way to do this is to say, "Go home and get some sleep." A more effective way is to ask, "Would getting rest right now allow you to do the work you need to do in a state of energy and not exhaustion?"

By telling someone they have the equivalent of a nail in their head, you might find you're crossing a relational boundary saying the thing that cannot be said—but it needs saying, and the sooner you can touch the suffering point, the better.

Domino: Everyone has a different background that shapes who they are and how they see the world. That background, along with their current life conditions and circumstances, make up their emotional atmosphere. Learning a person's emotional atmosphere can help you understand and connect with them much easier.

Questions for you: What are the atmospheric conditions in your life, creating suffering of some form for you? What are the atmospheric conditions of those you want deeper connection with?

CONNECTION AND DISCONNECTION

When I was a freshman trying to navigate the high school landscape, I did my best to be a pain detective who was kind and helpful. But despite my efforts, I felt disconnected.

When I became a sophomore, I started getting high. I took a ceramics class that year and to my surprise, I loved it. Shy and introverted, I didn't like to play sports, I didn't like theater, and I didn't like most of the other clubs at the school, but I knew one thing: throwing pots was cool.

The combination of the wheel spinning and my hands shaping the chaos of wet clay into something solid made hours pass like minutes. I forgot my problems and flowed with the clay. I liked ceramics so much that I stuck with it for three years.

As I got older, I got more into drugs and partying as a coping mechanism for all the hard emotions I dealt with. Working with clay helped me numb some of my pain, and I became less inhibited, more outgoing, and more confident.

Gradually, I had more people around and became popular, but I didn't feel very close to my friends. We smoked or drank together, but we weren't developing the kind of deep bonds I was really looking for.

Even if I didn't know it at the time, my ceramics class was *connecting* me to myself, and the drugs were *disconnecting* me from myself. Though they seemed to have a similar effect in dealing with my pain, they couldn't have been more different.

The important thing to notice is that when we're in pain or suffering, we want to find a way to feel connected to alleviate that pain no matter what—but how well that works and what its results will be depends on the intention behind it. To a large degree, it depends on how grounded or "connected" you are with yourself. When you're self-connected, you'll feel like you're enough and you can *give* to the world around you. If you're disconnected from yourself, you'll feel broken or like you're not enough, and it'll result in *taking* in order to close that gap. In my case, it was *taking* drugs and alcohol to numb the pain or *seeking* approval and status from association with others, versus *giving* my creativity to the world through doing ceramics.

It can be tricky to tell the difference because it's often not about the actual thing you're doing, it's more about how and why you're doing it. You can *give* outrageously expensive gifts to the most popular people in your field to make others think you're generous, but it will only be self-connecting if you actually *are* generous in other ways as well. I've seen countless people donate to charities they could care less about, just to make themselves look good and hide their otherwise unethical backgrounds. If you know you're not like that and you're just trying to fool people, then your "giving" is actually *taking* advantage of people.

The point is not to overthink or overanalyze everything, but to be aware of the nuances of connecting and disconnecting from people. To truly *connect* with other people, you have to be okay with yourself on a basic level, whatever your flaws may be. You can be charming and suave when networking with other people, but if you think at your core that you're not worthy of those people or that you always *have* to be charming because otherwise people will see the *real* you that you don't like, people will feel that. You will feel disconnected from yourself, and eventually, other people will probably feel disconnected from you as well.

Not everyone has to deal with addiction the way I did, but the principle of moving toward connection and away from disconnection in yourself *and* with others is valuable for everyone. The truth about creating strong relationships is simple: everyone wants to feel connected and nobody wants to feel disconnected, but to get the connections you're looking for, you have to feel connected with yourself as well. Finally, telling the difference between real connection and disconnection can take presence, patience, and practice.

> **Domino:** Being connected and being disconnected can sometimes feel similar, but they are very different. Search for activities and people that allow you to feel your emotions in a safe way, and avoid activities that push your emotions away or make you dissociate.

> **Questions for you:** Which activities are deceptively disconnecting you from yourself? Which activities are genuinely connecting you to your core self?

TRUST, RAPPORT, AND COMFORT — WHY YOU NEED ALL THREE

Connecting with people requires a balance of trust, rapport, and comfort, and even if they all sound roughly the same, they're actually quite distinct. While this topic is usually about building trust, rapport, and comfort with others, it applies equally to your connection to yourself. Do you trust yourself to succeed? Do you have "rapport" with yourself (think of this as a sense of humor—finding yourself funny)? Are you comfortable with who you are?

Perhaps one of the most famous voices on the subject of rapport—with others and within yourself—is my friend Neil Strauss, who wrote *The Game* and *The Truth*, the latter of which I collaborated on. In *The Game*, Neil follows a community of pickup artists in Los Angeles and documents their relationships with one another as well as how they interact with women. At one point, the book offers a simple formula for making connections with other people: "Rapport is trust plus comfort."

Though it might seem strange to take a definition of rapport from the world of pickup artists, the truth is, individual intentions aside, few people have broken down how rapport works in as much detail as that group of people did. Funny enough, the reasons behind how and why they were able to do so have a lot to do with suffering and the difference between self-connection and disconnection.

As Neil has written and discussed over the years, he grew up without having much experience with women and came to assume that he just didn't have "it"—meaning whatever natural charm it was that made some men successful with women while others weren't. He first found out about pickup communities from an editor who wanted him to write a how-to book based on their teachings. Neil refused, as he was a serious journalist—but because he was lonely and curious, he entered the community under a pseudonym with a hope of becoming better with women to improve his self-esteem. Over time, Neil became so interested in the people he met and learned so much about their world that it resulted in the book *The Game*.

After meeting the people he profiled in *The Game*, Neil realized that the "it" he thought he was missing didn't really exist in the way he thought it did when he was growing up. It wasn't one thing, it wasn't something you either had or didn't have, and it wasn't magic. "It" was actually a set of skills, and they were skills that could be *learned*.

In the communities he wrote about and learned from, the people he met were able to break down the concept of rapport building in so much detail mostly out of necessity. Many of them had felt alienated throughout their lives, which had led to pain and loneliness. As a result, they had both a deep need to escape from their pain and a powerful motivation to learn how by connecting with other people. (As a side note, it should maybe come as no surprise that many of the people who dabbled in these communities in the early 2000s later became great marketers!)

The nuanced part of this story is that learning to connect externally without doing the internal work to come from the right place still *does* work, though only to a degree and only for a while. Unfortunately, inner disconnection can still catch up with you eventually. As Neil has explained himself in books and interviews over the years, his own insecurities and fears were what drew him so deeply into the world of *The Game* in the first place. What has been said less often—but I can say here as Neil's friend—is that his self-awareness and dedication to personal growth were what made him decide to leave that world behind.

Neil wrote more about that decision in *The Truth*, a book about processing your own childhood pain and finding a sense of self-connection in order to have healthy, fulfilling, and sustainable long-term relationships. It is essentially a sequel to *The Game* that finishes the story by telling the other half: that it can be dangerous and even harmful to use powerful external skills to charm others without coming from a grounded and self-connected place yourself.

Though the reputation of "pickup artistry" has changed over the years (and you may have better uses for your time than trying to seduce as many people as you can), the underlying psychological principles those communities explored are still instructive—both in relationships and in business.

You don't have to be perfectly accepting of yourself to learn how to connect better with others, and connecting with others likely *will* help you become more self-connected. Just remember: the intention behind how you use your rapport-building skills to connect with others matters, and it can quickly flip into extreme disconnection if you don't remain aware of it. In talking with Neil about what his experiences through *The Game* and *The Truth* taught him about rapport, he summed it up as simply as possible: using rapport to connect with people is great, but using rapport to manipulate is wrong. For more on rapport building and self-esteem, you can listen to a longer conversation between me and Neil on www.JoePolish.com/WIIFT.

However we come to it, *rapport* is what we're ultimately aiming for in our interactions with other people. Once you have rapport, it means you get along. You know the other person likes you and thinks you're worth talking to.

The problem most of us have is knowing how to get to that point—and all the missteps we make along the way.

Should we make more jokes?

Should we ask more questions?

Should we laugh harder at *their* jokes?

Fortunately, the formula mentioned above helps answer the question. In order to have rapport, you first develop comfort and trust. And of those two, comfort must come first.

Comfort is a relatively easy thing to understand: it means that someone else has a feeling of ease and freedom with you. It means they're not afraid of you suddenly screaming or swinging at them. It means they know you won't intentionally say the wrong thing to embarrass them and their friends, that you're attuned to their feelings and needs.

Comfort can be established relatively quickly by paying attention. But what about trust? That takes time.

In some sense, in fact, trust is "comfort plus time." We may feel comfortable with a person in the moment, but how do we know that they're not just on their best behavior?

What if what they're showing us is a front?

What if they're trying to get something from us by being funny or nice or helpful?

In truth, deep trust can only be established over time, because time proves a person's reliability. Still, like comfort, you can earn at least *some* trust from people in the short term by not behaving erratically, being rude, breaking people's boundaries, and so on.

Not surprisingly, a lot of this comes back to pain detection—though there's still a caveat to that: you can only know so much from a first impression, no matter how empathic or observant you are.

Some people are easy to read, but with others, it takes time and experience to see them entirely. And sometimes, you may not like what you discover. Plenty of people who seem charming and charismatic at first glance turn out to be manipulative, narcissistic, and, in some cases, just plain dangerous to be around.

Even in those situations, learning to be a pain detective will help you determine where you should connect and where you should disconnect. It will help you learn how to proactively ward off and disconnect from people who are takers, leeches, and energetic vampires before they can harm you!

This is not a matter of if, but when.

In business and in life, you absolutely will get manipulated and taken advantage of. But with practice and intention, you can develop keen pain detection abilities, which are a deep form of discernment. You'll feel and see if a connection brings comfort, trust, and eventually rapport. You'll feel very quickly if the other person is a giver or a taker, if the connection is transformational or transactional.

To do that, you can take a few key actions. Many people do these things unintentionally already, but to really assess a situation, you can use them a bit more intentionally:

- When meeting new people, don't just talk about yourself and your own accomplishments—**ask them questions**!

- **Don't be afraid to mention a weakness or shortcoming** before mentioning your strengths. This makes you more relatable and likable and helps build trust.

- **Pay attention to your body language**—smile often, look people in the eyes, stand at an angle to people you're speaking to so that your presence feels less confrontational.

- Once you've established a little comfort, **make a joke**! *(Even if it's a bad joke!)* Socializing is supposed to be fun, so don't be afraid to lighten up a little.

- **Speak a bit more slowly** than you normally would. Speaking too quickly is usually a sign that you're nervous or insecure, which can make people uncertain about you.

- **Ask people for a small favor very early on** or do them a small favor very early on. Depending on the situation, either one can endear you to them.

- **Validate people!** If someone tells you how they're feeling, don't try to correct them or suggest they're exaggerating. Just acknowledge their feelings.

- **Be honest about your own feelings and intentions.** People can tell what you think and feel by your body language, so don't be afraid to actually tell them.

While every situation is different, applying the principles above in conversations with people will make you feel grounded and help you to create rapport quickly. And once you've done that, all that remains is for you to keep showing up for that person again and again over time.

Domino: Trust, rapport, and comfort are all required to connect with others—and even if they seem similar, they are entirely distinct. Fortunately, all three can be developed.

Question for you: Where can you build greater trust, rapport, and comfort in a key relationship today?

BE INAUTHENTIC AT YOUR OWN PERIL

In thinking back to the younger version of myself, I can see a pretty clear arc now from the smiling four-year-old to the shy and awkward high schooler to what came next. Spoiler alert: what came next wasn't pretty.

My efforts to keep up a happy front and signal happiness all around had created positive effects on some of the world around me, but my front was masking what was going on inside—and I wasn't sharing it with others, either.

People weren't learning about what had happened with my mom, what my life was like at home, or that I'd been raped, molested, and paid not to talk about it, beginning at about nine years old.

Instead, I was learning that even though I wasn't good at sports or academics or theater, I *was* good at taking drugs and partying. Eventually, I was high all the time. I didn't even attend my high school graduation. Instead, I watched it from a friend's backyard while we freebased cocaine.

After graduation, I freebased and snorted cocaine every day for three and a half months, selling drugs to support my habit. I was five feet ten, and after hardly eating anything for a week, I was down to 105 pounds. On one occasion, I drank alcohol, smoked cigarettes, smoked pot, snorted cocaine, freebased cocaine, snorted crystal meth, and took LSD all in the same day. I had become a full-blown drug addict, and my life was beyond a mess.

In the middle of it all, I knew I had to get out of Arizona or I was going to die. Eventually, I packed up my stuff and drove to New Mexico to live in a mobile home trailer with my father. To do so, I cut off all my old relationships and tried to get sober (which turned out to be a grueling six-month battle).

After a two-year string of odd jobs, 12-step meetings, and a lot of exercise, I was discovering that I didn't want to work for anybody. Instead, a friend convinced me to spend my savings—all $1,500 of it—on equipment and supplies to start a carpet cleaning company. And that's what I did.

Between hauling equipment out of cat-piss-soaked apartments in un-air-conditioned buildings in blazing summer heat, I found myself questioning my decision. After all, I was allergic to cats. And no matter how hard I worked, I was sinking deeper and deeper in debt.

My strategy changed after a friend of mine invited me to go Jet Skiing with a couple of guys up at Saguaro Lake. He said that a successful real estate investor would be there, and I thought I might learn something from him (even though I was so broke that taking a Saturday away from work was hard).

At the lake, I explained my situation to this man sitting on the tailgate of a pickup truck—how I wasn't making money in carpet cleaning and wondered if there wasn't a better business to go into.

"Does anybody in your business make money?" he asked.

I told him that a few people did.

"Then the business isn't the problem. You're the problem." As I drove home that evening with a bad sunburn, I came to the conclusion that he was right. I was just as capable as anyone else. I had survived my childhood, after all. Surely, I could make a carpet cleaning business work.

After reading more books about business and systems thinking, I learned about systematizing the best parts of a business to make it work more efficiently. With that, inspiration struck.

I would systematize the part that made me money: marketing.

I hired a copywriter with borrowed money because I wanted to replicate and clone my message, and we wrote what would become my first sales letter, the *Consumer's Guide to Carpet Cleaning*. It contained the most important things I had learned about how to hire an ethical carpet cleaner, sure, but it was more like my applied thesis on being a pain detective.

Hiring an ethical carpet cleaner wasn't a particularly easy decision, after all. My strategy would not be to trick or coerce the customer. Instead, I wanted to teach them and help them. I believed if I was the one to educate them, they would have trust and rapport with me. I was going to give them value before I asked for anything.

From a business point of view, it worked. Within six months, I went from grossing $2,100 in an average month to grossing $12,300. At that, I stopped thinking only about cleaning carpets and shifted my focus to messaging and marketing, and my business continued growing from there.

The larger point, though, is if you can sniff out suffering, you can sniff out problems people have that need solving, and if you can solve those problems, there is no limit to what you can do. It is the cornerstone of business and life. By identifying pain points and making positive space for people, you open the door for transformation. Good marketing applies this seamlessly: identifying and connecting with the pain of the other person, connecting with their bigger future, and being the bridge.

There may be no magic-bullet argument for why you ought to care about other people, but I can try to give my version.

For one thing, I have a goal to create more grateful, empathetic, generous, value-creating human beings. Though we live in a world of suffering, I want to lessen it at scale—and the crazy thing is that even if that's positive for other people, I still benefit greatly from it too. In fact, it's the entire reason I created Genius Network in the first place!

On the other hand, being genuine and positive for me still comes right back to what I was investigating as a kid. It is all about energy.

By being kind and positive, you get to put positivity in the world and watch it ripple out. As you do it more and more, those ripples get bigger and bigger and they start echoing back toward you—and when they do, there's no telling what it will mean or how it will transform your life. When that energy comes back, it can create situations that are exhilarating, humbling and even terrifying. For me, it's the most exciting thing there is.

It's how I want people to use this book as well: to design the best outcomes for themselves and for others.

All I know for sure is that I'm driven to reduce suffering. It may very well be the meaning of my life—at least, it's the meaning I strive to create.

Domino: There is no magic bullet strategy to connect with 100 percent of people all the time, and taking a strategic or mercenary approach to relationships is often a losing strategy. Instead, be authentic with others — because being inauthentic will hurt you in the long run.

Questions for you: Where are you being inauthentic in your relationships? Where can you muster the courage, today, to be more honest and authentic?

The Dominoes:

- To be better at life and relationships, learn to ask, **"How are they suffering, and how can I help?"**

- When facing problems in life or relationships, remember that *everyone* **is suffering in their own way—and often more than you realize.** This will increase your empathy, create opportunities for relationships, and much more.

- **Suffering is at least partially a matter of perspective** and our mindset in dealing with it. In full view of our suffering (on whatever scale), we still have choices.

- **Suffering can be useful** if it creates opportunities for connection.

- **Be a pain detective** to connect with others. Focus on the other person and their suffering first. You and your possible solutions come second—not the other way around. In other words, this book will not be popular with people who want to focus only on themselves. This book is *not* for narcissists and takers.

- Everyone has a different background that shapes who they are and how they see the world. That background, along with their current life conditions and circumstances, make up their **"emotional atmosphere."** Learning a person's emotional atmosphere can help you understand them and makes connecting with them much easier.

- **Trust, rapport, and comfort** are all required to connect with others—and even if they seem similar, they are entirely distinct. Fortunately, all three can be developed.

- There is no magic bullet strategy to connect with 100 percent of people all the time and taking a strategic or mercenary approach to relationships is often a losing strategy. Instead, **be authentic with others—because being inauthentic will hurt you in the long run**.

Exercises and Action Steps

1. The Pain Detective's Three Magic Questions

To get to what matters, you have to see behind the façade many people put up.

If you really want to help someone, you should be a root farmer, not a fruit farmer. Being a pain detective means getting at the root.

To do this, I like to ask people three great questions I got from my friend Ken Glickman way back in 1991:

1. Where are you?
2. Where do you want to go?
3. How are you going to get there?

These are great for finding out what makes other people tick and how you can help them, but they're also great to apply to yourself. Just as other people can put up a façade with us, we can do it to ourselves as well.

In short, anything you want in your life, personally or professionally, can be achieved by starting with these three questions.

2. Create Your Genius Network

Years ago, I heard someone say that if you can't write an idea down on the back of a napkin it's probably not worth doing. Later, I heard a line from the late copywriter Gary Halbert: "Any problem in the world can be solved with the right sales letter."

I'm going to add to that wisdom and say: "Any problem in the world can be solved with the right Genius Network"—which is simply a network of people who have skills, capabilities, and genius you can access whenever you need a connection, idea, or solution. People who can help you solve problems, meet challenges, and reach opportunities.

Now, while learning how to create Genius Networks may sound like a great tool, you may also be wondering: *What does that have to do with suffering?*

What I would say is that connecting with other people is almost always about relieving pain on some level, even if that pain is relatively slight in the grand scheme of things. On the extreme end, think of two lonely, sad people who happen to meet, get along, and become friends. They now have a two-person "network" that helps alleviate their loneliness. While a friendship of proximity is definitely not a Genius Network, a Genius Network still operates by some of the same principles.

In a Genius Network, everyone in the group is well connected, wants to give to others, and probably has some other external markers of success, whatever that means to them. On the surface, it may seem like those people aren't in much pain or don't have problems—but that's simply not true. Sometimes their problems are smaller by comparison (the "pain" of not knowing how to hire a great employee for their business, for example), but sometimes the problems are as big as they come (such as the pain of hiding a fatal illness from your family and the fear that comes with it).

In other words, an average network and a Genius Network are not all that different in terms of the underlying motivation, because both can help you solve problems and create better experiences for yourself and others. The main difference is a Genius Network is much more *intentional*, with people who come together to solve *specific* problems with the shared intention of *giving* to one another rather than simply taking.

When I want to solve any problem in the world, or reach any opportunity, or overcome any challenge, I ask myself who the very best people would be whom I could invest my time, money, and energy in. To do that, I use this Genius Network tool and mindset to force my brain to search for solutions.

The idea of Genius Network isn't something that just falls into your lap. It's about *becoming* a Genius Networker who *does* Genius Networking so they can eventually *have* a Genius Network.

So, what do I mean by that? An easy way to think of it is with a simple exercise:

1. Take a piece of paper and draw a circle in the middle.

2. Draw eight smaller circles in a ring around it.

3. In each of the smaller circles, write the name of one of the eight most important people in your life.

4. Under their name, describe their skills and capabilities.

5. Now think about how you can help each of those people. And think about how they can help you.

It's interesting to see what happens when you are forced to narrow your list to eight people. Who comes to the surface?

As this exercise helps show, Genius Networking starts with being thoughtful and learning how to be valuable to the people around you. After that, it's about connecting and spreading that value across a network—and finally, it's about using that network to solve problems. The right Genius Network is always the best tool for solutions.

To use the tool, first identify an area you want to improve, a relationship you want to grow, or a problem you want to solve. Next, identify the most valuable relationships you have in your life, what they want, and the capabilities they have. Finally determine how you can be most helpful to them.

As Dan Sullivan said on our *10xTalk* podcast: "You should never expect any opportunity to be given to you unless you give value to other people." It is why you must think about what you can do or offer to others to be genuinely useful to them (the key word here is *genuinely*).

It means not being attached to outcomes or needing others to do something for you. For it to work, you can't have a one-sided "taker" agenda.

In essence, the "My Genius Network" tool forces you to think:

1. Who are they?
2. What do they want?
3. What capabilities do they have?
4. What do I know and what can I do to be most useful to them?

Though this is a powerful tool, it can't be used as a gimmick. If you don't come at it authentically, you miss the entire point.

This capability only works long term with someone who has developed their character and good intentions and who follows through with congruent action. It is a tool that works to the degree you involve yourself with it authentically and engage with it. If you are willing to do that, it will be very valuable to you.

Chapter 2

INVEST TIME, ATTENTION, MONEY, EFFORT, AND ENERGY IN RELATIONSHIPS

I've been many different people and lived many different lives, yet I'm most known as the founder of Genius Network.

Genius Network is a high-level entrepreneurial group and connection network with the goal of building better entrepreneurs to change the world through ELF (easy, lucrative, and fun) businesses. The group connects and collaborates with the world's brightest business minds, creating momentum to contribute to one another and the world.

In short, Genius Network is about investing in yourself, your business, and your relationships to make as positive an impact on the world as possible. Being a member requires a significant financial investment, from $25K to $100K a year.

There are plenty of people who can't afford to be in Genius Network, of course. But nearly everyone I meet wishes they could be better at forming and maintaining strong relationships. This is a life skill that is essential for everyone—and available to everyone.

The first secret to the successes I've had in life and business is simple: I invest more time, attention, money, effort, and energy into my relationships than I do anything else, and I do so on the longest timeline possible.

WHAT ARE RELATIONSHIPS AND HOW ARE THEY FORMED?

My good friend Dr. Robert Cialdini is the author of numerous game-changing books including *Pre-Suasion* and *Influence*. He is known globally as the most prominent expert in the science of influence and how to apply it ethically in business. He is incredibly knowledgeable about relationships. As Dr. Cialdini explained to me, having a connection with someone involves bringing *collaboration* to the experiences you create with them.

Dr. Ned Hallowell, my friend and psychiatrist, and the author of over 20 books, called connection the true Vitamin C. In *Driven to Distraction*, a book that was foundational to the modern understanding of ADHD, written with co-author Dr. John J. Ratey, Hallowell affirmed that connection is something all of us literally need to survive.

To paraphrase these two geniuses as simply as possible, a relationship is a *collaborative connection*.

Connection and collaboration allow you to combine your capabilities, concerns, communication, context, comprehension, compassion, and caring with another human being to create something new. Relationships are fundamentally creative and, in a sense, even artistic.

Defining "art" may be too big a task to take on in this book, but we can agree generally that art is a mode of expression, whatever form that may take. An artist is a person who has the power to *express*. And this is where things get interesting.

Whether singers, actors, writers, performers, or athletes, many of the world's most admired people are incredibly *expressive*. Their respective art can stir huge emotions in the people observing them, and it's not an ability limited to what we typically think of when we think of art. Incredible entrepreneurs can be corporate artists. As an example, CEO Steve Jobs became great in large part because of his artistry in marketing, packaging, positioning, and leadership.

Relationships are about connection, and connection is about *expression*. It is about being open, communicative, and free with the people around you about what you want and how you will get there together. The most connected relationships are aligned in purpose. In some cases, purpose can come out of joy, like two people who share a passion for painting and push each other to experiment and be better. Other times, purpose can come out of pain; it is a major part of what 12-step recovery is all about.

No matter what the common bond is, connection is the key to relationships. Of course, navigating that emotional landscape can be treacherous.

Domino: No matter your expertise or interests, relationships are a life skill everyone can work on mastering.

Relationships are about connection, which is about expression. By being open and expressive, you align with others in purpose for greater impacts.

Question for you: What is one common way you've seen people you admire being expressive and open that you feel uncomfortable doing yourself — and what's stopping you from pushing yourself to try that same behavior in one of your key relationships today? (Examples could include public speaking, singing, doing stand-up comedy, art, music, dancing, etc.)

INVESTING VERSUS SPENDING IN RELATIONSHIPS

You've heard the saying "time is money." To me, and to anyone who defines true success as being happy and accomplished in the world, *relationships* are money. The distinction is important, because many people who are financially successful are incredibly disconnected from others—and they're some of the unhappiest people you'll ever meet as a result.

In many ways, building businesses and wealth and building relationships go together because the best thinking behind them is so similar: you have to be a long-term investor to see real results.

Creating great relationships, like creating great wealth or social impact, begins with your mindset. People who view relationships as transactions act like they are in the transaction business. People who view relationships long term behave like they're in the relationship business.

Another way to think of transactional versus transformative relationships is the difference between *spending* and *investing*. They may sound similar, but they are completely different. Spending refers to the necessary costs of an undertaking, costs that are often unpleasant. Investing is adopting a long-term mindset and accumulating positive, generative energy.

A spending mindset doesn't work when you want to meet and befriend the right people: burning through relationships via short-term, transactional exchanges leaves you depleted. The only way that pattern can sustain itself is by finding greater and greater numbers of people (i.e., victims) to take advantage of, but it usually catches up to the person doing all the taking. When people act this way, it's as if they're treating every interaction with people they meet like an overnight stay at a cheap motel they were forced to stop at on a road trip. Life may be a journey, but at least some of the people we meet along the way should become our travel companions.

The investing mindset is like frequenting the local restaurant where the owner knows your family, the staff are your friends, and you don't look at the menu because the server knows your order.

Investing time, money, and energy in relationships means looking at everyone as an investment, not a cost. It's nuanced, because being too stingy or unwilling to spend your time, attention, money, effort, and energy won't result in the rich life and deep relationships you want, but neither will spending those resources thoughtlessly on anyone who crosses your path.

As in all things, you need a good framework to be effective. Fortunately, when it comes to relationships, the framework you need is just one sentence long.

Domino: The best relationships are formed from the perspective of *long-term investment* rather than short-term spending. The resources you spend or invest in relationships are your time, attention, money, effort, and energy.

Questions for you: Where are you being short term and transactional in your approach to important relationships? What would shift if you took a longer-term investment approach?

THE ONE-SENTENCE SOLUTION

In 2000, Ben Hunt-Davis captained the British national men's rowing team. Ben gave the team a question to ask before every decision made and every action taken in and out of practice: "Will this make the boat go faster?" If the team considered going to the pub the night before training, they asked themselves, "Will this make the boat go faster?" If the answer was no, they did not go. (Here's a tip: if you have to ask, the answer is usually no.)

With the difference that one question made in their behavior, they won gold at the 2000 Sydney Olympics. To go for gold in your relationships, you can use the same strategy.

Before doing something, ask yourself: *Does this grow the relationship?*

Establishing a connection is great, but good relationships are also about *growth*. After you've planted a seed of time, attention, money, effort, and energy, you can't just walk away. To see it grow into a tall tree with a thick trunk, you need to keep watering and tending to it.

The caveat, of course, is that *not all growth is created equal.* You can grow a mighty oak tree or you can grow a cancer that invades every vital organ. Not all growth is progress, and not all growth is helpful. The key is to make sure your relationships are mutually beneficial, rather than destructive, after you pour in your resources. As you dedicate yourself to growing trees, you'll have to routinely check that they are producing fruit. It is a lesson I've learned the hard way again and again in my own life, beginning in high school.

During my partying days, my relationship with my friend Fred was like the movie *Fast Times at Ridgemont High*. Fred drove a VW bus and we went off campus to get lunch and get high. The first red flag came when Fred drove off, leaving me alone in the parking lot. I shook it off, assuming he was just playing a prank.

A few days later, I was walking to my locker when I saw someone coming toward me from the side. As I turned, Fred punched me right above the eye and I fell to the ground. He jumped on top of me and as he threw blow after blow, all I could think was: *Fred and I were supposed to be friends*.

The relationship Fred and I had might not have been deep, but I had invested plenty of time, attention, and energy in it. And our friendship had grown in a destructive way, into him feeling comfortable jumping me in front of my locker.

I learned an important lesson from this about who I chose to spend time with. The good news is, you don't have to wait until you're getting pummeled by a so-called friend to evaluate the relationships in your life.

- If you are funding a start-up, is it progressing as you invest more and more into it? Or are the founders burning your money and attention without yielding anything in return?

- Are your strategic business partners opening new doors and showing you new opportunities?

Or are you funneling business to them at great personal expense?

- In your friendships, do you feel equally supported and respected? Or are you perpetually listening to other people's problems and extinguishing their fires without them lending you a willing ear in return?

The lesson for how you deploy your time, attention, money, effort, and energy is simple: Relationships have a built-in feedback mechanism called *growth*. Any relationship, positive or negative, will develop and grow as you invest more and more.

The question is, are you growing together in the right direction? Or are you spiraling off into the darkness? What are the by-products or fruits of the relationships? What internal and external transformations is it producing? Ignore the feedback that growth offers at your peril. Make the choices that make the boat go faster.

> **Domino:** Evaluate your actions in relationships with one sentence: Does this grow the relationship? Growth is a feedback mechanism built into relationships that reveals their health — but growth can be positive or negative. Cultivate positive growth and cull negativity.

> **Questions for you:** What are the most transformational relationships you've ever had? What growth was produced through the relationship?

DEEP RELATIONSHIPS MAKE THE BIGGEST IMPACT

The impact your time and energy have on the world around you depends a lot on how they are applied. If you're talking about an agenda someone else doesn't care about, you will see their energy deplete. If what you say and do puts wind in their sails, you will see them glow, buzzing with energy.

There's a spiritual component to the dynamic of the energy in our relationships and its impact on the world. We think of energy as stored fuel—like gasoline—but it's also a dynamic of expansion and contraction. Whenever you expand a person or situation's energy, you create incredibly powerful network effects.

One day, as I walked to my car a big guy with a shaved head approached.

"Joe Polish?" His tone was soft. "Good to see you."

"Do I know you?" I asked cautiously, noticing how muscular he looked.

"No," he said, "but I'm a medical doctor and I listened to your Piranha Marketing audios almost twenty years ago." He was referring to a program we created in 2004 released by Nightingale-Conant called *Piranha Marketing: The Seven Success Multiplying Factors to Dominate Any Market You Enter.* "You were instrumental in helping my business early on. I don't want to bother you, I just want you to know that you changed the trajectory of my life. You never know the impact you make on people."

His lesson really surprised me. It's easy to focus on what good relationships can do *for* you, but what about the other side of the equation? What about what you're doing *to* or *for* others? It's like the saying almost everyone has heard before: "Be nice to the people you meet on the way up; they're the same people you'll meet on the way down." I've shared this quote with so many people over the years.

I treat everybody I meet as if I will run into them again. As much as I can, I want to make a lasting impression and whenever possible, leave everything better than before I showed up. The most positive impacts I've made haven't been overly calculated strategic decisions. They have grown organically out of this simple philosophy.

The bottom line: Spread as much positivity and love as you can wherever you go, not to avoid some imagined future punishment, but because you don't know the magnitude of the impact that positivity will have on others and the world. Usually, our humble efforts have an effect reaching farther than we think.

> **Domino:** A network of deep relationships create compounding, outsized impacts. This is the idea behind Genius Network, and you can apply the same principles to make your own networks.
>
> **Question for you:** What life-changing impacts have occurred in your life through other people, even those you never personally knew?

A RETURN ON GENIUS

So far, we've discovered:

1. You form relationships through deep connection, and deep connection happens through honest and open expression, investing your time, attention, money, effort, and energy into other people. The key is to invest these

valuable resources in the *right* people; to help with this, think of your resources in terms of energy contracting and expanding rather than as a fuel tank that's full or empty. Do your relationships expand or contract your energy? In return, how do you expand or contract the lives of others?

2. The measure of your relationships can be found in the built-in feedback mechanism of growth. Implicit in the word *feedback* is that what you put in comes back in some way, positive or negative. Strong relationships grow in a positive direction for both parties.

Now, let's add a third point that we stress in Genius Network:

3. There is a difference between a return *from* relationships and a return *on* relationships. Understanding the difference is key to figuring out how to allocate your time, money, and energy.

The first is a qualitative question: "If I were to invest time, money, and energy, would I get a return *from* this relationship?"

The second is a quantitative question: "Now that I've decided, how much time, money, and energy should I invest to get a return *on* this relationship?"

It's the difference between merely having high-quality people in your network and interacting with those people in a meaningful way. You are looking for a return on genius. And this is also why a Genius Network is so valuable. (That's why one of the exercises I asked you to do in the last chapter was to map out your own.)

By having a Genius Network of relationships in your life, you get to speed up your returns on relationships and tap into your network's latent genius capabilities in ways you could have never dreamed without a giving, adaptive, intelligent, and solution-oriented network around you.

Return on Genius could also be called Return on Reputation. If you're known as a useful, caring, generous person, that reputation compounds as you surround yourself with more people aligned to your purpose. It's a simple formula: *The more good you do, the more good you get.*

It's something I've been saying for years: *Life gives to the giver.* (It's also the title of one of my books, which you can get for free at www.JoesFreeBook.com.)

If you're giving people the right things, life will give abundantly back to you. If you're giving people the wrong things, life still gives back but it just might not be what you want to get.

Genius Network is a capability network, and the more capabilities you combine, the greater the probability that you get a return on the collaboration and connection of those capabilities. As anyone who has one can attest, a network of deep relationships can create compounding, outsized impacts far greater than we can make on our own.

Describing the work I do at Genius Network, member Jason Fladlien said, "You assemble unicorns." In isolation and surrounded by donkeys, unicorns are miserable. I find unicorns and introduce them to one another because together, unicorns change the world.

Domino: The benefit of having many positive, growing relationships is a Return on Genius, the latent capabilities and talents of your network. For this to work, relationships must be authentic and reciprocal.

Questions for you: What return are you getting on the investments you're putting in your relationships? Do you have your own Genius Network of continual returns?

THE 12 DANGERS OF INVESTING IN RELATIONSHIPS

All the groundwork we've looked at for how to connect, invest your energy, develop relationships, and make huge impacts in the world has to do with the good side of relationships. Of course, there are potential downsides. Working a 12-step program helped me with addiction recovery and changed the way I view myself and the world. As an homage to that, I've compiled my own list of 12 things to avoid in your relationships—ways you can unknowingly invest your time, money, or energy in the wrong ways. All of these are traps I've fallen into myself, so I know. You can hear a lot more on these topics in podcasts and interviews I've done with some of the smartest people around—check them out at www.JoePolish.com/WIIFT.

Time Dangers

1. **Putting your desires, growth, talents, and capabilities at someone else's mercy.** This happens when you don't understand what you're good at or when you haven't developed the skills to have freedom and autonomy. Know the difference between practice and

performance. A professional athlete spends infinitely more time practicing for the game than playing the game. In the stages of life where you're learning, developing, and trying to create mastery, you have to be willing to learn to be skilled with your time. The danger here is that after you do all the reps, you need to switch gears and recognize your own value. If you never adopt the identity of a professional, you'll be stuck with mediocre relationships and results even though the skill and potential are there.

2. **Overcommitment.** The more visionary or creative you are, the easier it is to think you can do more than you can. Hone your ability to analyze how much time a project takes. A rule that works for me is: when starting any new endeavor, factor in how much time, energy, and money is required. Then double your figures. Big undertakings usually take twice as much effort as you think they will. If I had learned this earlier in my career, I would have saved myself a tremendous amount of heartache. If you're realistic about the resources you'll need to commit to a given project, you can become increasingly selective about what and who you say yes to.

3. **Disorganization.** If you own or consume too many things, the stuff spiraling around requires your constant attention. Be careful of accumulation. Do the things you own actually own you? When you spread your time and attention thin, it becomes impossible to go deep

with anyone or on anything. Instead, you can only go shallow. And when investing in relationships, deep is always better than shallow. Invest where the returns continue to multiply.

4. **Always saying yes.** When you're in opportunity mode, a Not To Do List is more important than a To Do List. Early in life, it's good to be eager and jump at opportunities, but doing that too much or for too long takes you far off track. Knowing ahead what you won't do saves time, reduces energy spent making decisions, and allows you to focus on what's most important in life. Work toward saying no to more and more. My friend Derek Sivers says, "If you're not feeling 'Hell yeah, that would be awesome!' about something, say no."

Energy Dangers

5. **Lack of sleep.** How do you solve one problem that in turn solves 5, 10, or 100 problems? You get more sleep. When you solve your sleep issues, you have multiplied energy and focus, which solves countless other issues in your life. Don't underestimate the power of sleep.

6. **Poor nutrition.** How you fuel your body is critical. The food you eat, your water intake, and your movement are vital for energy. Like other living things, to be healthy your body needs water, nutrition, movement, and extended time outdoors. As your health improves, the quality of people around you does as well.

7. **Being in the wrong environment.** When you put yourself in the wrong environment, your surroundings can drain you. When you get yourself into the right environment, it can energize you. Is your environment life-giving? Is your environment positively evolving you?

8. **Leeches, parasites, and fake friends.** As you become successful, having the wrong people around you leads to low energy, overextension, codependence, misalignment, and guilt. When things go well, everyone is nice so they can benefit from your success. But when things are difficult, pay attention to who shows up. There will be people in your life who are great when you're at their level, but if you become more successful or grow beyond them, they quickly become your nemeses. Invest your energy in people who show love, appreciation, and want to support you no matter what. Sorting the fake friends from the real can require deep work.

Money Dangers

9. **Reckless spending and gambling.** Episodic or sporadic spending is the opposite of being strategic. When it comes to managing money, avoid a gambler's mentality. Do your due diligence on where you put money or crypto. Invest in people you can trust without fear. Steer clear of people with bold promises but red flags.

10. **Not protecting your money.** Money must be managed and protected. This means getting insight into insurance, legal structures, and taxes. Over the next decade, wealth will be made and lost gambling in the cryptocurrency and blockchain world, not to mention on things we haven't yet seen. (As I write this book, NFTs are all the rage, but by the time you're reading it, who knows?) Invest in relationships that are collaborative, and avoid relationships that are obviously risky.

Above is a Cryptopunk, one of the earlier high-profile sets released in 2017, from my own NFT collection. Can you see the resemblance?

11. **Being flippant with debt.** Know the difference between money you've earned and money you've borrowed. One of the greatest killers of success is not owning your own future. When your future is actually being funded by somebody else, don't flippantly act like you're entirely in control. Borrow wisely

and from the right people, or you'll find yourself in debt to the wrong people.

12. **Trying to impress others.** Are you buying nice
cars, houses, clothes, or status on social media
when you don't have the money to afford it?
At the root of this is jealousy and insecurity
about other successful people. This attitude
can lead to delusional thinking or financial
recklessness. Rely less on money and more
on wit, talent, and connecting with the right
type of people. Sustenance is more valuable
than portraying a false image. Anyone who is
status-focused is a red flag to be avoided.

These 12 tips shine a light on the major landmines
to avoid as you forge your way in the world. Each has the
potential to become your kryptonite. They may not all
apply to you, but knowing which ones are your personal
dangers will help you immeasurably in the long run.

Domino: When maintaining relationships, nearly all the
biggest dangers and traps come from mismanaging
three things: your time, energy, and money.

Question for you: Which of the 12 dangers is most relevant to you?

FINDING YOUR FLOW AND YOUR FUN

My friend Dan Sullivan asks people if they have ever gone
for a swim in the ocean. As people raise their hands, he
says, "When you came out and someone asked you how

was the swim, do you say, 'Well, it was a good swim, but I missed a lot of the ocean'? How much water do you need when you go swimming?"

When everything in your life is about compounding value or multiplying opportunities—when you're worried about getting *all* of the ocean—you can become transactional without noticing. It's what would happen if you loved spas because of how relaxing they are and then tried to open a spa business. Suddenly, you wouldn't be able to relax anymore. Part of mastering relationships is about finding your flow, using your time productively to get what you want, and managing yourself without getting depleted.

In one of my many interviews with billionaire Richard Branson, he said when he works out one hour a day, he mentally and physically feels like he gains an extra four hours of productivity. When you get your relationship recipe right, that's how your investments of time, attention, money, effort, and energy should feel.

There is no perfect way to build relationships without some mistakes, no right list of the people to know. We are always missing opportunities, and there are always ways we can better leverage our time. At the end of the day, though, are you happy? Is your life working? Are you learning and expanding yourself? Most importantly, are your relationships *fun*? They're supposed to be. People hang out with people they like. People do business with people they like. People may do business with people they don't like, but usually because they have no other choice. As soon as they have options, they will find the people who can solve their problems *and* make them feel good. It is true no matter where you go.

As much as life is about connecting with others, it is also about *disconnecting* from what doesn't serve you. As you go through this journey, realize that you always have the power to walk away. Also notice when other people are *walking away from you*, particularly if it's a repeating pattern.

If you don't want people to walk away from you, be a caring, useful person. Be the person others want to connect with. As you get more experience and success, you will be surprised to learn how many of life's games are simply about kindness, openness, and collaboration.

These are all skills that can be developed. How do I know? Because growing up, I was one of the shyest, most introverted and awkward kids. I was afraid to talk to people. I had super low self-esteem. But I realized that if I kept making myself useful and kept learning, I could overcome some of my fears. I never dreamed how far that desire would take me. I learned to be useful and caring. You can too.

Domino: To keep your relationships in perspective, focus on finding your flow rather than following a specific set of rules. Above all else, relationships are supposed to be fun.

Question for you: How can you make your relationships more fun and flowing? Where can you remove the needless friction?

The Dominoes:

- No matter your expertise or interests, relationships are a life skill everyone can work on mastering.

Relationships are about connection, which is about expression. By being open and expressive, you align your purpose with others for greater impacts.

- Being connected and being disconnected can sometimes feel similar, but they are very different. Search for activities and people who allow you to feel your emotions in a safe way. Avoid activities that push your emotions away or make you dissociate.

- The best relationships are formed from the perspective of **long-term investment** rather than short-term spending. The resources you spend or invest in relationships are your time, attention, money, effort, and energy.

- Evaluate your actions in relationships with one sentence: Does this grow the relationship? Growth is a feedback mechanism built into relationships that reveals their health—but growth can be positive or negative. Cultivate positive growth and cull negativity.

- The benefit of having many positive, growing relationships is a Return on Genius, the latent capabilities and talents of your network. For this to work, relationships must be authentic and reciprocal.

- When maintaining relationships, nearly all the biggest dangers and traps come from mismanaging three things: your time, energy, and money.

- To keep your relationships in perspective, focus on finding your flow rather than following a specific set of rules. Above all else, relationships are supposed to be fun.

Exercises and Action Steps

1. What Needs Solved?

To get a Return on Genius, first go back to the Genius Network list of the various geniuses in your life that you built at the end of Chapter 1. Next, identify a *problem* in your life that needs solving, one that you can't solve by yourself. Use an exercise I call *What Needs Solved?* that asks these four questions:

1. What problem needs to be solved in your life?
2. What would your life or business look like if you were able to solve that problem?
3. What would the three biggest benefits be of solving that problem?
4. Who do you know who can help you solve the problem?

The first three questions are important for you to get clarity, and the fourth question puts things into motion.

Remember the lesson of the chapter: you have to *invest time, attention, money, effort, and energy* into relationships to achieve the greatest successes in life. Doing so requires you to take real action to connect with other people, and this is an easy and effective way to start.

2. The Not To Do List for Relationships

As the time, money, and attention dangers lists show, sometimes success in life isn't about what you do, it's about what you *don't* do.

Everyone has a limited amount of time. Once spent, there's no way to get time back, but we can stop spending time on things that take us away from our purpose. In the past, I've advised people to create Not To Do lists in their businesses to identify time wasters so they can stop doing them. You can do the same thing for your relationships. Here's how:

1. **Which of your relationships come easiest to you and who do you most love to spend time with?** These are the people who will help you live an ELF (easy, lucrative, and fun) life, so they should take up a majority of your time. Write down five or six examples.

2. **Which of your relationships help you grow the most? Which ones make you the most money?** These two lists may be slightly different, because sometimes people push us forward as human beings without making us a lot of money—and sometimes, our relationships with people keep us restrained in certain behaviors but make us rich. If you see a significant difference between these two lists, what can you adjust to bring who you love spending time with and who you make money with into closer alignment?

3. **What are your top three goals for your relationships in the next 90 days?** After

comparing your answers to 1 and 2, you should have some ideas about how to reallocate your time so you spend it with more ELF people who *also* make you money. If all the people who are ELF for you don't make you money, one of your goals can be to find people who are—or find an ELF idea for the people you enjoy most.

4. **What <u>action steps</u> can you take toward those goals?** Define the steps to achieving your goals and *do* them. Following through is up to you, and will show in your results.

5. **Now that you know all the above, which relationships should you invest *less* time, attention, money, effort, and energy on?** The relationships you write here will lead toward a HALF (hard, annoying, lame, and frustrating) life. Write down five or six relationships.

6. **How can you create boundaries in those relationships to preserve your time and energy?** We often still have to have some relationships that are not as ELF for us, but nobody said you have to let those relationships take over your life. The goal of this exercise is to spend as much time as possible with people in list 1, and to make list 1 convert into list 2. For everything else, do whatever you can to set boundaries, communicate clearly about your needs, and preserve your time. And remember: one person's HALF is another person's ELF.

In a business, you may have things shared between 1 and 2 that you're good at and that make you money but still aren't ELF for you. Similarly, in relationships, there can be people in 1 who you're *comfortable* with who are still holding you back or harming you, or people in 2 who make you a lot of money but you can't stand.

There's no one-size-fits-all for relationships, so use this information carefully. Not everyone you like spending time with needs to make you money, and you don't have to love the experience of hanging out with everyone who helps you grow. There is a place for an aggressive personal trainer when you're out of shape.

All the same, use this tool to get a picture of your most impactful relationships.

3. The Not Now List

The exercises above are designed to help you identify and list your problems on paper and to create some rules and boundaries for your relationships so you can focus on solving them. Still, even if you have some idea about where you should spend your time, it's easy to get off track or disorganized (especially for entrepreneurial people with so many ideas bouncing around in their heads that they can't keep them straight).

Trying to juggle your life goals while overhauling your relationships, becoming more self-connected, and learning how to be a pain detective to relieve others' suffering is a lot to do all at once. In fact, taking on way too many projects is often a way to guarantee that none of them get done the way you'd like them to in an ideal world—and that stress can even create *more* unnecessary suffering for yourself and others rather than less.

For these reasons and others, using a Not Now list can be helpful to get each of those different pieces of your life in order. I first heard about this great concept from my friend and best-selling author David Bach, and I liked it so much that I turned it into a tool, which I've used for many years to help with overwhelm and deciding what to do when. To put it into action, answer the following questions:

1. What are my biggest priorities right now?

2. For things that are not current priorities, what ideas, opportunities, people, projects, and tasks are still worth tracking?

3. If pursued and invested in, what value, impact, or result will those things create?

4. Comparing your current priorities to the other list, what insights do you have?

In this exercise, there is less of a right and wrong involved; it's a question of time management. Similarly, there's no built-in judgment attached to your current priorities versus the less urgent things you're putting off, but you might make those judgments yourself when you answer question 4.

Is there anything you overly prioritize? Are there relationships and projects that would lead to more of an ELF life that you keep putting on the back burner? Use this exercise as a way to reflect and make changes accordingly.

Chapter 3

BE THE PERSON THEY ALWAYS ANSWER THE PHONE FOR

One day, I got a call from an acquaintance of mine, a wealthy woman who had been married to a very wealthy businessman. When I saw her name, I was more than surprised. We hadn't spoken in eight years!

I answered, and after some small talk, she explained that I'd been in a dream she'd had. In her dream, I had appeared with her husband, shaking hands and laughing. As she explained, her husband had died the year before, and she wanted to know if I had ever known her husband in real life. I said that I hadn't—but I couldn't leave it at that, because it was clear that she was in a very fragile state. After chatting for a while longer, she said she wanted to see me again, and we agreed to meet for dinner at a high-end resort in Arizona where she was staying.

In person, I realized my acquaintance was in an even more fragile state than I'd realized. She was also under tremendous pressure.

In the wake of her husband's death, she was dealing with lawyers buying people off and countless other people trying to cut in on the pot of money her husband had left behind. All the businesses she and her husband had co-owned were still functioning under their own management teams, but it was a precarious situation that was too much for her to handle.

As we spoke, two things became very clear. First was that in her vulnerable state, it would've been so simple for people to take advantage of her. The second was that it was special that she called me to talk to, because she could've called anyone.

This woman was incredibly traumatized, but she was also incredibly wealthy, which created a very difficult situation to navigate. Even though she was in real pain and needed help, she couldn't share that pain with just anyone. After all, it was a perfect opportunity for takers and predators to step in.

Toward the end of the conversation, the woman explained that she wanted to help other people in recovery. She had been in recovery herself for a while, but I sensed that this new pressure would make sobriety hard to maintain. I told her I felt that reaching beyond her focus on recovery wasn't the right move for her at that moment. Instead, she had to focus on herself. Before she could make an impact, she had to get better first—because in a fragile state and with a big pot of money in the balance, she had a target on her back.

As we parted ways, I introduced her to a brilliant psychiatrist from Genius Network and asked him to talk to her for free as a favor. Throughout our interaction, I didn't want anything from her; I just wanted her to get the help she needed.

On the way home, I was still scratching my head about why she called me (or why I appeared in her dream). I remembered that when we first met I had given her some contacts and numbers for people I knew who could help her and her husband. As I mulled it over, I realized that whatever I had said or done eight years before had stayed with her and made an impact on her life.

> **Domino:** Even though humans need solitude and deep connection with themselves, we are ultimately social creatures. It feels reassuring to connect with others because we are *designed* to.

> **Questions for you:** Do you have any connections in your life today that you could deepen to improve your life and theirs? Is there anything stopping you from doing so?

WHO IS WORTH ANSWERING THE PHONE FOR?

In the modern world, we have more connections than ever spread farther apart than ever before. It means a lot of "relationship upkeep" happens on our phones (or, by extension, our social media messages), which makes it a good proxy to measure your and others' character.

Of course, part of that comes from my own life experience.

After I lost my mother, I felt very alone as a child. Every one or two years throughout childhood, my father would uproot my brother and me from wherever we were living and we would move—and usually we tended to move when he was anxious or depressed. With my mom gone, he never felt settled anywhere, so he had to keep moving.

The result was that I was forced into a lot of short-term relationships—and while the quality wasn't there, I tried to make up for it in *quantity*. Even so, it started to feel like a losing strategy.

While juggling so many relationships, I found myself wanting deeper and more profound connections with people. To do that, I knew I had to focus on spending less of my time and energy on anybody who wanted it and more on the *right* people. I didn't know which of the many connections in my life were actually with the right people and worth nurturing, but I knew I needed a way to figure it out.

By accident, I started uncovering some clues about which connections might be those right people I was looking for—all thanks to the invention of caller ID.

Before caller ID, when someone called you, all you knew up front was that someone somewhere wanted to talk to you about something. As a social, friendly person, you would answer the phone whenever it rang and then find yourself in conversations with people you didn't really want to be in. With caller ID, everyone suddenly had a choice about which calls they wanted to pick up or not!

As I got used to the new technology, I noticed that I tended to answer the phone for people who had good energy. People who were joyful, excited, friendly, and caring. And similarly, the people who often picked up the phone for me felt that I gave them that same energy in return.

When talking to *those* people, conversations flowed smoothly and nobody felt like they were trying to be somewhere else. If things got unexpectedly deep, that was fine—they were still conversations both people wanted to be in, and the relationship would grow as a result. To me, a simple rule came out of it: I had better, deeper connections with people I wanted to answer the phone for—and becoming that kind of person was a skill anyone could practice.

This advice is incredibly straightforward, but it's because it works! When you're trying to get a project off the ground, who do you want to spend more time with—the person who is excited about new possibilities and who can inspire you to push your idea even further, or the person who discourages you from even trying or tries to sabotage your project out of jealousy?

In a social setting, which one do you prefer: someone who has empathy for other people and cares that everyone else in the room is getting along and having a good time, or someone who only cares about themselves and is oblivious to everyone else's feelings? I could go on, but you get the idea.

To live a truly ELF life, you need to be able to screen and sort through people to find the ones who are positive to be around—the ones who are worth answering the phone for. But being in a position to choose has to start with you doing the same work on yourself. In other words, other people will also have to want to pick up the phone for you.

The simplest way to be this kind of person, in addition to embracing some of the qualities I mentioned above, is to focus on being *useful, grateful, and valuable* to people according to their situation (which we'll cover more deeply in the next chapter). Still, the reality of doing that is a little more nuanced.

We tend to think of being caring or friendly or whatever else as an objectively "good" thing to be, but the truth is people are more complicated than that. Not *everybody* immediately trusts someone who is overly friendly—but some do. Not *everybody* loves someone who is constantly cracking jokes, but some do appreciate a little levity. And others, including myself, enjoy some really twisted humor!

Being the person others answer the phone for means balancing three things:

1. Knowing who you are and what you like at a core level

2. Knowing who other people are and what they like at a core level

3. Being able to adapt in a way that both you and other people can enjoy and benefit from in a wide range of situations

Though these principles are simple, they can be tricky to apply between people who are very different—especially the third point. For example, how can someone who lives their whole life by the book and someone who is completely spontaneous find common ground? Won't one of them feel out of control and the other one feel way too boxed in?

We tend to gravitate toward people who are either like us or who are doing things that we like. In both cases, it helps to think of people like mirrors. The positive characteristics we see in others are things we think we already have—or they are things we think are underdeveloped in ourselves. Similarly, their "negative" characteristics are the shadow parts of ourselves that we haven't accepted.

As you see these differences between people in your life, it can be a good reminder to go inward and question why there's friction. What is it about how someone acts that bothers you, and what does that say about who you are as a person? What does it say about who they are? Is it possible that you don't know the answer? Maybe you should ask!

By turning that initial conflict into genuine curiosity about someone else's life and ideas, you open the door to connection. In turn, that sense of generosity creates a better connection and a greater space for mutual understanding and tolerance of one another's differences, leading to a more enjoyable experience for everyone.

In the best cases, it may even mean growing into a more well-rounded person by developing some of the qualities you were initially scared of or even repulsed by!

These kinds of constructive interactions between people remind me of Dan Sullivan and Ben Hardy's book *The Gap and the Gain*. In their book, "the gap" is the difference between what you are now and what you think your potential is. Of course, everyone has heard that they should "reach their full potential," but nobody actually does. Whatever potential you achieve just unlocks new potential. As Dan says, you can see the horizon, but you never touch it. And the same thing is true with any idealized character traits you have in your mind. They are good to aim for to get started on a path, but you shouldn't fixate on them as ends in themselves. Instead, you have to realize them by actually *doing* things.

Twenty years ago, I wrote a prescription for how to have a great day. In it, I gave a bunch of basic steps and instructions, but the details don't matter for you right now. What's important is how it ended:

> If none of this makes you feel any better, go visit, or better yet volunteer at, a children's hospital, AIDS clinic, or nursing home. You'll immediately have a whole new perspective on how to have a great life and how great life really can be.

The truth is, the best way to remove character flaws isn't by overthinking everything you're doing. The best way is to move your own light into the darkness and try to help other people.

> **Domino:** To connect, be someone others would "answer the phone for." In practice, this usually means being caring, kind, and curious — but more accurately, it means giving energy that people are attracted to.

> **Questions for you:** In your life, who are the people that you would always answer the phone for and what kind of traits do they have in common? Who would always answer the phone for you?

ATTRACTION AND REPULSION

My friend Gary Halbert, the late great copywriter, told me that one of the most important things you can do with customers and your marketing is *bond* with them. He thought it was so important that he named one of his sons Bond!

I got this lesson from our many conversations and from Gary's newsletters early on because I'd been reading them for years as one of my main sources of marketing information. His letters were a simple eight pages in black and white, folded into a number-10 envelope. There was something about that combination that made me want to open them immediately when they came in the mail.

Gary wrote in an inspiring way that felt like he was talking to my desires and my goals. He was basically a hardcore, smart-ass guy who taught hard-hitting, result-producing marketing methods. He was a powerful teacher who used the written word like a magician to convey concepts and teach things. The fact was that his emotional style of writing created a *bond* with me. He created an energy that *attracted* me to his message.

Ultimately, the spark of those connections we're all looking for comes from some kind of attraction—and the absence of connection comes from repulsion. The tricky part comes down to something my friend and former dating coach Eben Pagan says: "Attraction isn't a choice." What this means is that we all find different qualities in people attractive or repulsive depending on our own backgrounds. We are attracted and repelled by people based on shared interests, values, characteristics, and even senses of humor.

My friend and love coach Annie Lalla, also the wife of Eben, added her own insight to that idea: "True love is 50 percent attraction and 50 percent repulsion." The point Annie is making is that the deepest connections involve not just our "attractive" qualities but also the darker traits of our shadow. When someone falls for you, it might be due to a shared value, but more often it's something that they lack! In human relationships as in marketing, the best results come from working with that push and pull and keeping the two in balance.

For me, I am attracted to people who are resourceful, who are achievers, and who have good character. I seek out people who have a sense of urgency and who have done the work to transform themselves, especially people who had difficult upbringings that they overcame. Those people are way more interesting than the people my friend Dan Sullivan says were "born on third base but grow up thinking they hit a triple."

Of course, I am also attracted to people who will do the right thing in hard situations, and doing the right thing is very different from doing things right. After all, there may be a *right* way to rob a bank, but robbing a bank isn't the right thing to do. There are right ways you can make money with marketing, but taking advantage of people, or flat-out lying, or overhyping things are all examples of the wrong ways.

To combine Eben and Annie's wisdom, I would put it this way: I can't help being attracted to both high achievers and very kind people, ideally when they're describing the same person! However, the reality is those two character traits are often opposed and create constant tension in the people who have to balance them.

The point is not that you *have* to be more patient with people you don't relate to or that you *should* strive to be more balanced. Everyone has those different sides that are always pushing and pulling, within themselves and with others. Understanding that for what it is rather than idealizing people lets you be a fuller version of yourself—which is like flying a signal flag that the people you need to balance you out can see.

Domino: We are all attracted to certain energies, and attraction is not a choice. That can mean that you are naturally pulled toward energies and people who are not good for you and your life.

Question for you: What kinds of people and things are you most attracted to and why?

WHY ARE PEOPLE ATTRACTED TO DANGER AND PAIN?

In good circumstances, following the things you're attracted to is a good thing—but without any introspection, it can be a weakness. Of course, sometimes, you might need to take a second look at what you're attracted to.

There's something important I've learned by studying marketing: *you are not your own customer.* In short, this means that the things *we* think make us or our product most attractive are often not the same things that other people find attractive about us or our product; sometimes, we market what *we* want, not what other people want.

There's an important lesson there for relationships as well. Even though people might say they are looking for nice, friendly, inviting, courteous, caring, and fun people, they often pursue dangerous, narcissistic people who are insulting to them.

How can that be? Why is it that people who are downright abusive liars can still have fans clamoring to meet them, take pictures with them, vote for them, and support them? If they're so repulsive on paper, why are people so attracted to them? (Human nature is fascinating.)

One way of looking at it is that if everyone agreed about what constituted a "great person," all of us would vote the same way, act the same way, and so on. In fact, all of us have different values shaped by our experiences, and they determine what kind of people and experiences we seek out.

To use a food metaphor, we all have different taste buds. Some people like broccoli more than spinach, or French fries more than bananas. Even so, there is a big difference between how something *tastes* going down and how much it actually *nourishes* us.

With food as with people, taste and preference are debatable; the nourishment part, less so.

Why are some people attracted to danger, pain, and dysfunction? It's too deep a question to answer completely here, but there are plenty of possible reasons.

There's a psychological theory about "trauma bonding" that tries to explain this phenomenon. I'm not a psychologist, so I leaned on my friend Ken Wells, who is a world-class addiction therapist, to help explain it:

> Trauma bonds originate with damaged attachment during childhood development. Every child has developmental needs to be addressed—touch, mirroring value, predictability, and knowing that they matter are just a few.
>
> When these needs are met in a satisfactory way, secure attachments are formed. This leads to a sense of belonging and safety, an ability to self-regulate, the capacity to form intimate connections, and the ability to separate and create boundaries from those who are close to us.
>
> When those needs are not met, we end up developing into a chunk of Swiss cheese, riddled with holes. We need to fill those holes (our unmet needs) from the outside by getting power, position, and control through accomplishments and others' approval. Thus, "trauma bonding" is when

two people who are riddled with holes form an unusually close connection with one another that doesn't serve either one of them.

Fritz Perls is famous for saying, "Nothing ever changes until it is real." To heal trauma and avoid trauma bonds, you must come to a place where you recognize that your relationships with toxic people are an attempt to fill a psychological need that was never addressed as a child or grieved as an adult.

When we get victimized as children, our resting or "normal" state is one of instability and chaos. It means that when people around us act selflessly, with healthy boundaries, or in a way that respects us, we can get suspicious (even if we know, on some level, that we need more of those people in our life).

It also means that the initial "spark" of attraction we sometimes feel with people out in the world can be an extension of that trauma bond: we recognize something of ourselves in those people. Maybe the people we're seeing are also victims—or maybe they're abusers who will re-create life situations that we're used to.

The point of saying all these things is not to blame anyone for "choosing" wrong or to shame anyone; it's to illustrate a bigger point. Human beings often gravitate toward whatever they know, no matter what it is, unless they make a conscious effort to become aware of what they really want.

Domino: Some people enjoy, pursue, and become addicted to danger and pain in relationships because of their experiences. Even so, shifting away from those behaviors and energies can be done and is better in the long run.

Questions for you: Do you have any friends who often lead themselves into dangerous or painful situations in a way that follows a pattern? Why might that be? Do you ever find yourself in dangerous or painful situations in your own life as a result of your own beliefs and experiences?

HONE YOUR PEOPLE PICKER

There is a popular speaker who used to tell a story about how he got into a car accident. As he explained, after the accident, he was sitting in the road bleeding and he had an incredible insight about the value of his own life. At the end of telling the story, he started crying onstage.

When I first heard him tell this story, I was impressed. *This is so authentic!* I thought. As I got to know him better, I saw him tell the story again and again and noticed that he cried after telling it the exact same way every time, which I found strange.

Eventually, after speaking to his friends and people who worked for him, I learned that the story was manufactured and was based only loosely on real events. It was designed to evoke sincerity without being sincere—but he had told it so many times that even he had gotten caught up in the drama of it and believed it to be true.

Though I'd been attracted to this person's energy and story, and we had become friends, I had to end the relationship after I realized that the way he presented himself onstage and the way he was and the way he did business offstage were totally incongruent. Ultimately, this person was more of a taker than a giver, no matter how good a first impression he'd made on me.

Most people have a cautionary tale like this from their life, though it's often from when they were younger. For me, this was relatively recent! It was a good reminder of the importance of honing your people picker.

So, what does that mean, exactly?

Just as we have the senses of sight, sound, taste, touch, and smell, we also have some "people senses" that are just as critical. When the way you pick people is messed up, you end up wanting to connect with people who are the equivalent of junk food, but you may only realize it after you are sick.

Because so much of my life is about marketing, it's hard not to relate this people-picker concept back to it as well. In relationships of all kinds, people are sometimes afraid to "market themselves" to get what they want, but the truth is, we are *always* marketing ourselves whether we want to or not. Our behavior and communication style with others *is* our marketing—in effect, it's an unconscious part of our "people picker" because it is what helps other people assess if they want to spend time with us. With that in mind, it's definitely in our interest to try to bring those things under our conscious control!

In business relationships, not doing so can mean "attracting the wrong clients." The same can be true of friends we choose to spend time with, especially if they only bring out our negative traits or self-destructive habits. Maybe most pointedly, it even applies to romantic relationships and our ability to find love, which I explored by using what I knew about marketing to write a personal ad that might find me a soul mate (as strange as that may sound).

I first came across the idea after talking to a friend who used his copywriting skills to write a singles ad for himself as part of an online campaign. His campaign included explicit statements about his political beliefs and preferences for a girlfriend, and it included a lot of humor and personality. Because it was so direct and honest, it was also seen as provocative, stirring up a lot of attention and media reactions and eventually going viral.

Even though his approach wasn't particularly focused on finding a soul mate, per se, it still got me thinking about how people used marketing principles even in their romantic lives. With that floating around in my mind, I remembered an e-mail from Annie Lalla, the best love coach I've ever met, in 2015 that came somewhat out of the blue. Here's how it read:

Joe,

This is important. You keep visiting my thoughts. My intuition knows that we need to talk and yet I've been avoiding it, not sure why. But I can see through that fear now, so I'm proactively asserting my idea in this email.

I feel called to write, mostly it's because I know Eben loves you but also I think your heart has the war-torn characteristics of someone whose gone through enough pain, to be capable of one of the most epic love stories ever experienced by a human, I don't want you to die without experiencing what I and Eben see as the highest game a human being can play with their life: True Love.

I want you to know the feeling of being loved exactly as you are, down to the bone before you leave this world. The knowing that you are able to fully give and receive the highest quality of love possible; this is what true spirituality is about.

I think I can help you, but only if you're willing to suspend belief in everything you've learned about how love works.

Let's build a new definition of what romantic love might look like for you—from scratch. Then we'll harness an immense amount of courage & faith into calling in a future romance that we'll design in your dreams. But you'll need to let go of all your fears, doubts, and cynicism.

This is not just for you but for all of mankind, because the human race needs YOU to be in love. Who you will become—in terms of impact and contribution—exponentially increases when your woman finds you and shapes you into your greatest self.

Joe, you deserve to be in love, let me help you. I was made for this and so were you.

I'll love you either way—even if you don't respond to this invitation.

Tightest hug,

Annie

Annie and I had been great friends over the years, but I hadn't expected her e-mail and it completely blew me away. I had just started seeing someone, so I thanked Annie for her words without taking her up on her invitation.

Due to many different factors, I became single again around 2018. I remembered Annie's e-mail and reached out to start cautiously stepping into the invitation she'd offered.

As Annie and I had started working together, we'd had many conversations about love and relationships and all the different beliefs I had about what love was and how possible it might be for me. I sometimes drew on what

I knew about marketing in our conversations, to which Annie commented that the highest possible use of marketing would be to find someone I could spend my life with, and that she wanted to be the "PR agent for [my] heart."

With everything we had been discussing in mind, Annie and I worked together to write a new kind of personal ad grounded in my core beliefs and my best self. After putting a lot of thought into it together, this was the ad we crafted for my future soul mate:

> *I'm not interested in changing you.*
>
> *I want you to relax into being who you most want to be.*
>
> *I'm here to protect and encourage the parts of you that are creative, intelligent, fierce, and tender. I'll be your sanctuary and your trampoline.*
>
> *What I want is a woman who's devoted to something so important, she's dedicated her life to it. I will devote myself to supporting you there. Your growth and expansion will become our priority.*
>
> *I once read, "You don't fall in love with another person; you fall in love with who you get to be around them." I want you to feel the most yourself when you're around me. This will inspire me to do the same.*
>
> *I'm a successful entrepreneur with a wide array of passions. Committed to personal development and growth, I aim to add value to every person I meet. I create connections between powerful leaders and build networks of collaboration. My high-paced, intense lifestyle requires a strong woman who knows how to represent her needs and capitalize on once-in-a-lifetime opportunities.*
>
> *If you're proud of the way you love others, remain tender in moments of fear, and feel confident in your*

*ability to hold the pain of others, then we'll reso-
nate well.*

*It takes courage to be sensitive and honest when
life feels challenging. I need someone with this kind
of courage.*

*If you're in the top five most extraordinary women
you've ever met, then I want to meet you.*

I promise I will treat you like a queen.

But you have to already know that you are one.

The ad came out better than I could have imagined
and truly represented me. I recorded a podcast episode
with Annie on *I Love Marketing* to share the journey of
finding my soul mate. We ran the ad on a couple of dating
sites. I won't get into too many details about the results
of the ad and my personal life (though a fuller version
of the story is available in the *I Love Marketing* episode I
did with Annie, which can be found on www.JoePolish
.com/WIIFT). Suffice it to say that letting Annie be the
PR agent for my heart was one of the best things I've ever
done. It taught me as much about romance as it taught me
about connecting with people and was a reminder of why
I became interested in marketing in the first place.

Everyone comes into the world without any assumptions about how things are or ought to be. Over time, we
learn things from our experiences and the world around
us—whether good or bad. A lot of what we learn in life
happens so early in childhood that we don't even remember learning it, which makes it very hard to *unlearn*. On
some level, there are some experiences we have that are
so intense or formative that it's almost not possible to
completely "unlearn" them and they just become part of
who we are.

Understanding this can go a long way when it comes to building rapport with people and being someone that people answer the phone for. As much as this book talks about being kind or helpful to people, sometimes what that really means is communicating with people in a way that lets them know you see who they are and that who they are is okay with you. With some people that can mean teasing them, giving them shit, and challenging them rather than just being nice and supportive all the time.

Before you can even do that though, you need to understand that those people exist, you will have to interact with them, and there's a reason they became the way they are. Similarly, you have to understand that applies to *you* as well. Even if other people seem to seek out danger and inconvenience, there are probably places where we're doing the exact same thing to ourselves.

Once you can accept that, you will have a lot more choices. You can choose to empathize with difficult people and build rewarding relationships with them by communicating in a way they understand, or alternately, you can keep the people you *don't* want to connect with away by setting boundaries and communicating in a way that will repel them.

Refining those skills of rapport and connection can come in equally handy in business, friendship, and romance, as well as nearly any other subject you can think of involving human relationships. Still, to do so, you have to understand what's underneath it all: to a large degree and for better or worse, people are unconsciously at the mercy of their own habits and experiences.

With that being said, this doesn't mean we can't change our patterns or improve, because we can! What it does mean is that without examining our experiences and thoughts, we will likely keep finding ourselves in the same situations. For people who have had extremely negative or traumatic experiences, that can mean being attracted to people and situations that make you feel the same way because it's familiar (though the same principle is true for nearly all people, regardless of the specifics).

Understanding this can bring your life more under your conscious control, and can open you up to a much broader way of connecting and building rapport with other people. It all comes down to getting to know yourself—and knowing your criteria for the people you spend time with.

My 90-year-old friend Harvey Mackay wrote a book many years ago called *Swim with the Sharks without Being Eaten Alive*. That was a business book, but the metaphor is true everywhere: Life is like an ocean. As you "swim" through your day-to-day life, you will encounter all kinds of fish—and because the ocean is a vast place, you will also come face to face with some sharks.

After some painful encounters with sharks over the years—and suffering the consequences of sometimes picking the wrong people in love and in business—I had to look at how I was choosing people. It led me to learn about psychology, self-help, and deep personal development to find people who were expanders and not contractors, people who were ethical rather than unethical.

As I learned, doing the work to improve how you choose people has a lot more to do with unlearning than it does with learning. In the process, it becomes a lot easier to see why people put themselves in negative situations again and again—even if it doesn't protect you 100 percent of the time from making some of the same mistakes yourself.

Domino: If you had adverse experiences in childhood or hard experiences in life, you may need to "hone your people picker" or risk falling into bad patterns.

Question for you: How have some of the harder experiences you've had in life changed how you choose who to connect with?

THE NECESSARY COST OF HAVING YOUR OWN VALUES

Even for people who believe in being useful, grateful, and valuable to others, it can still be hard to apply and live up to those values in everyday life. Similarly, if you want to work on being someone people will answer the phone for by working on your people picker, it may mean spending more time with people who make you uncomfortable but who you know deep down are pushing you out of your comfort zone and into significant growth.

Everyone has heard the saying "do something every day that scares you." That saying is all well and good until it actually comes time to do those scary things— and growing your relationships in the ways you really want can require a level of vulnerability some people find very scary.

Going in, it helps to know that being someone other people always answer the phone for is a double-edged sword. To become that kind of person, you also have to be willing to "answer the phone" for other people—and you may not always like what the other person is calling about.

Being a person other people want to be around isn't about being perfect. More often than not, it's about being a person who recognizes their own strengths and has their own clear values, and who isn't afraid to show them and share them with other people.

The benefit of being that kind of person is people who like what you stand for will know who you are at a distance, and they will seek you out. The cost is that the opposite is also true: you will also be clearly visible to the people who don't like what you stand for, and they might seek you out as well.

All of this is only to illustrate the full picture of what you'll be getting into by living this way. To live a connected life full of deep relationships that can help you achieve your own highest good, determining your own values and following them consistently is a necessary and unavoidable cost.

In the process, you will make plenty of mistakes, and you will have to own them in order to grow and to show other people what kind of person you are. Fortunately, living with best intentions and taking responsibility for your actions tends to attract other people who are trying to do the same thing.

When it comes to how you live your life, I think of the quote from the late American statesman Bernard Baruch: "Those who mind don't matter, and those who matter don't mind."

Still, as important as it is to show up in the world doing your best for others on the outside, we don't get the kind of connections and results we want until we do the work on the inside as well.

Domino: Defining your own values and living your life by them will still lead to making mistakes and having others judge you—but it is a necessary cost of forming good relationships and living your best life possible.

Question for you: What are the core values that you would want to live your life by, and how can you "market" those values to the world to connect with others?

The Dominoes:

- Even though humans need solitude and deep connection with themselves, we are ultimately **social creatures**. It feels reassuring to connect with others because we are *designed* to.

- To connect, be someone others would "answer the phone for." In practice, this usually means being, caring, kind, and curious—but more accurately, it means generating **energy that people are attracted to.**

- We are all attracted to certain energies, and **attraction is not a choice.** That can mean that you are naturally pulled toward energies and people who are not good for you and your life.

- If you had adverse experiences in childhood or hard experiences in life, you may need to **"hone your people picker"** or risk falling into bad patterns.

- **Despite best intentions, it is still possible to overextend yourself.** Be careful not to "move too far into darkness" to shine a light—or at least make these decisions carefully.

- Defining **your own values and living your life by them will still lead to making mistakes** and having others judge you—**but it is a necessary cost** of forming strong relationships and living your best life possible.

Exercises and Action Steps

1. Take a Fearless Inventory of Yourself (and Others)

Whether it's in ourselves or the people we choose to spend time with, characteristics are about character.

As Socrates famously said, "The unexamined life is not worth living." In that spirit, if you want to live life to the fullest through many deep relationships, you must understand how you operate with other people, unlearn the habits that don't serve you, and design better ones.

It's easy to point the finger at other people when things go wrong, but it's a little dishonest. If you keep bringing chaos into your own life, there's probably an issue with how you're behaving as well.

It begins by taking a "fearless inventory" of yourself, the kind that have been popularized by 12-step programs. Here's a simple way to get started:

1. **Get a piece of paper and make a list of your resentments as well as your character strengths and weaknesses.** Listing it all on paper removes resistance and lets you see yourself clearly. Look hard at your answers to get a better understanding of how you show up, what you like, what you don't like, what turns you on or off about other people—and, crucially, what you do that turns other people on or off.

2. **Next, write a list of questions and spend some time answering them and reflecting:**

What causes me pain?
What am I overly sensitive about?
What am I not sensitive enough about?
What am I biased toward?
Based on my life experiences, where might
I have some blind spots?

3. **Finally, look at your answers and write down explanations from your past about why you wrote what you did.**

    Did you learn some of those things from your family?
    From romantic relationships?
    From friendships or your environment?
    Make detailed notes.

4. **With all your new information, write down what you learned about yourself—and how you will plan to lean into your strengths and be more aware of your weaknesses going forward. Put your plan into action immediately.**

A phrase commonly used in 12-step rooms for that phenomenon is "what is hysterical is historical." It means that if you overreact or underreact to something, that reaction is tied to something that happened in your past.

So, ask yourself: Where am I overreacting and putting in way too much energy? Where am I underreacting? As a way to connect more deeply with these areas, if you need to, breathe, meditate, do therapy, or exercise.

After you've looked at yourself and done the work you need to do, *then* you can take an honest look at the people around you. For this, I have an exercise I take people through called "Your Purpose in Life."

Start by getting a blank sheet of paper and listing six people total: three people you know and who know you, and three who you know of but who don't know you. It doesn't matter if they are alive or dead or even lived in this century.

Next, list things three things you admire about each of them (for a total of 18 qualities).

Although it seems like a simple exercise about people around you, what it really reveals is what qualities *you* want in your own life.

2. Phone a Friend

It can be fun to theorize and speculate about how to be a more interesting and valuable person, but an even better way to get access to this information is to ask.

To find out what qualities of yours make others answer the phone for you, write down 5 to 10 people in your life who would answer the phone for you anytime, and ask them directly:

- What is it about you that makes them so loyal to you?

- What are their favorite qualities about you?

- On the other hand, what qualities do they find in other people that make them not want to answer the phone?

With this information, you should have a much clearer picture of the things you're doing right that other people admire about you—and the things other people do that you should avoid.

3. Write Your Own Personal Ad

To understand the power of using marketing-style thinking in relationships, you can do what I did with Annie
Lalla by writing your own personal ad, which can essentially be a "sales letter" for yourself. If you're already in
a loving relationship, you can still do this exercise for
friendships and other connections (or to start a conversation, have you and your partner both fill out personal ads
and compare them!).

However unusual or superficial that advice might
sound at first glance, before judging it, I recommend
remembering what I said earlier about marketing and
sales: they are not good or bad in themselves, and how
they affect others depends on a person's *intentions*.

For more on how to do this with advice from Annie
Lalla herself (plus a bonus Genius Network presentation
on love and how to connect and disconnect from relationships given by Annie Lalla and love expert Amy Chan),
visit www.JoePolish.com/WIIFT.

BE USEFUL, GRATEFUL, AND VALUABLE

O n one level, connecting with other people is something we have to do in life in the same way we have
to breathe and drink water. Many of us might value alone
time, but you won't hear many people say they want to
live a completely disconnected life. To live happy and
meaningful lives, being able to feel connected to others
and to our lives is a basic need.

The other benefit of connecting with others, though,
is that it leads to *being* connected, which is where things
get tricky. It's part of why I hesitate when people call me
"the most connected man in the world" or any version
of that, first because it's probably not accurate, and second because it's not always clear what the person saying
it means by it.

"Being connected" can have a negative connotation
to some people—suggesting social climbing or being
insincere—but in reality it's a lot like marketing or selling:

it is not inherently good or bad, and it all depends on how you use it and what your intentions are.

In practical terms, it's almost never a bad thing to "be connected." More often than not, it can help you accomplish your goals faster and with greater impact (and ideally those goals will include helping other people and pushing humanity forward). The point is that to be truly connected, we have to strive to improve our ability to connect *at will*. We have to be able to connect with anybody, anywhere—even if we won't always *have* to or even *want* to, we should still have the ability.

There's no one type of person we should all meet and form relationships with, but to achieve big goals, it helps to be connected to at least some high-achieving people, and some of those people tend to be wealthy, powerful, and "successful" in the traditional sense. Of course, to ward off others who only want to take from them, these people also tend to have their guard up the most.

With that said, how do you do it in what seem like the hardest circumstances? When you can't offer the other person a paycheck or an invite to some exclusive event? To put it as simply as possible, you do it by remembering that they are human beings with pain and insecurity just like anybody else.

The specifics can change, but in virtually any situation, being *useful*, *grateful*, and *valuable* are the three keys to connecting with others—and they never depreciate or go out of style. The secret is to know what will make you seem useful, grateful, or valuable to someone in any given situation. It's being *tuned in* and *attentive*!

But this is all easier to see by example.

On August 24, 2021, I traveled to California to visit my friend Dave Kekich, who was very ill at the time and in hospice. When I flew into Orange County, my friend Tim Ringgold was the one who picked me up at the airport.

As an aside, Tim and I met at his first 12-step meeting in 2003. I was active in the local recovery scene, and since I was a trusted servant of the program in the area, Tim and I spent a lot of time together in his early days of sobriety. Since then, Tim has been very open about his recovery process and wrote *Sonic Recovery*, a great book about music therapy in recovery. All this to say, having a friend who will pick you up from John Wayne Airport is extremely useful, but in my case, it was a relationship 18 years in the making!

That same day, Tim and I went to Laguna Beach to walk around and catch up on things. As we talked, we were brainstorming ideas for Artists for Addicts, a program I'd started in 2016 that I wanted to keep developing as a way to shift the global conversation about addiction away from judgment and toward compassion, using art as a force for good.

I first shared my idea for the program with my friend Akira Chan, who is a filmmaker and Genius Network member, as well as another friend and artist named Jon Butcher. Within a few months, we all started making a short documentary about how art could heal trauma to raise awareness for addiction and recovery. The resulting film was *Black Star*, which won an audience choice award at the Illuminate Film Festival in Sedona, Arizona, in 2018 and helped Artists for Addicts auction off more than $200,000 worth of art to raise money for recovery education.

As I was walking with Tim, I realized that Akira and I had always aspired to keep the ideas we'd explored with *Black Star* and Artists for Addicts going, but we had become too busy with our various businesses and creative endeavors. Then an idea hit me. Right then and there, I pulled out my iPhone and started filming a video of Tim and me talking about his work in music and recovery, even demonstrating some of Tim's music therapy techniques with drums and rhythms on the beach.

I sent the video to Akira to see what ideas it might spark, not sure what it might lead to. Shortly after, Akira replied with a video of his own.

"I think it's time to expand the film, and Tim would be perfect," Akira said. "Let's have you come down and do some filming!"

Just like that, we were figuring out the next steps and Akira and Tim were connecting on logistics. Within two video messages, being "useful" was transforming into actual value and action! Within a month, they ended up filming a group music scene that became a part of our ever-evolving Artists for Addicts project alongside my foundation, GeniusRecovery.org.

For all of this to happen, at every juncture of our exchanges with one another, Akira, Tim, and I had to trade *utility, gratitude,* and *value* back and forth. What that meant exactly changed from situation to situation, and it also changed as we changed over the years. In the case of my friend Dave, who died on September 9, 2021, what I found most useful and valuable and was most grateful for in the moment wasn't money or opportunity. It was just the presence of a friend who could share the experience with me—and give me a ride from the airport.

> **Domino:** To connect in virtually any situation, focus on being useful, grateful, or valuable — or some combination of all three. Put another way, all three of these things deliver a *positive result* of some kind to other people.

Questions for you: How are you useful, grateful, valuable, tuned in, and attentive to others in your life? How do others demonstrate those values to you?

WHAT DOES BEING USEFUL, GRATEFUL, AND VALUABLE LOOK LIKE?

These are the three qualities that are invaluable to maintaining relationships and networks of relationships: **utility, gratitude, and value**. In practice, that means *being* useful, grateful, and valuable to others. So, what does it look like when someone is being useful, grateful, or valuable?

On some level, each of these things gets *results* of some kind for other people. It could be a physical or material result like more money (a form of value), a cleaner yard (something useful), or a better outlook on life (a form of gratitude). The range of positive results that can come from applying these principles is virtually endless.

To really understand each one, it helps to think of people who model these principles, or of examples from real life. For usefulness, I'll go first, since usefulness was what helped me start my career.

Being Useful

As you may recall, when I started making my advertising *useful* is when my career in marketing really started to take off.

My first and most effective sales letter I ever created (with the help of a copywriter) was the *Consumer's Guide to Carpet Cleaning* in 1992, which I mentioned earlier. To really get a sense of how useful that was, you have to take a closer read. The guide began:

Read this guide and discover:

1. *7 questions to ask a carpet cleaner before you invite them into your home*

2. *8 mistakes to avoid when choosing a carpet cleaner*

3. *Crawling critters and crud: A guide to the slime, grime, and livestock that are seeping, creeping, and galloping through your carpet*

4. *6 costly misconceptions about carpet cleaning*

5. *How to avoid 4 carpet-cleaning rip-offs*

6. *How to get your carpet cleaner to 100% guarantee their work*

7. *The difference between value and price*

While a general guide to carpet cleaning would have been good in itself, these specific points on each step of the process took the entire offering to the next level! This was before the Internet was accessible to consumers, let alone being used as a marketing tool, so people were actually calling me and requesting a copy of the guide. Eventually, I turned it into a free recorded message that lasted 10 minutes and taught listeners the entire written contents of the guide.

And what do you think many of the prospects did after they received the guide? They called me again and asked, "When can you do the job?" The important thing to notice is that they did *not* ask me "How much do you charge," because my ELF marketing system had already sifted, sorted, and screened my prospects for me.

By that point, they were already bought in. Price would come up eventually, but their choice to work with me was already made.

*　*　*

In a business context, being useful in the minds of your prospects and clients as the best choice for their needs is a good way to make money and be successful. But in a personal context, the principle works the same way.

In day-to-day life, you want to position yourself as a useful person to other people in any number of ways. While most people might be thinking of being "useful" as someone who has a truck they can borrow to help them move apartments or someone who has access to a pool, being useful goes far beyond that (though it might include a truck or a pool as well!).

While having hard skills and material assets can be undeniably useful to others, what is *truly* useful varies from person to person and can change depending on context. While your utility has a lot to do with what you can bring to the table in terms of skills, it really begins with being concerned and conscientious—with caring about other people.

It starts as an awareness in your mind of other people's needs, wants, and pains, and it continues with identifying what you could add to an interaction to address or alleviate those things. It also involves true listening, which not everyone knows how to do.

It's something Dr. Cheri Ong, a board-certified plastic surgeon who operates a concierge medicine practice, has broken down better than anyone I know in a method that has three steps:

1. **Active listening.** Instead of waiting for your turn to speak, stay engaged the entire time someone talks to you. Ask questions and re-state things to them if you need to, just to make sure you understand their problems as if they were your own—inside and out.

2. **Empathize and don't overwhelm.** Understanding someone's problems rationally is one thing, but *feeling* for someone else and having them know that you empathize is much more effective. Second, though it may be tempting to offer solutions, talk about your own problems, or give endless information in response to a problem, don't overdo it! Otherwise, you will only add to their stress.

3. **Offer solutions that are simple to execute.** In personal relationships, sometimes a person just needs to vent, in which case, offering solutions or critiques isn't always needed. But in a professional context, a business context, or a personal context that is crying out for help, make sure your solutions are simple and can be implemented easily.

In her practice, Dr. Ong works with highly successful clients and does very intimate procedures, including vaginal operations. The conversations she has with her clients are some of the most sensitive, vulnerable, and private that two people could have. Since Dr. Ong is recognized as one of the top vaginal plastic surgeons in the world, she has had a lot of practice using rapport, compassion, and active listening in those conversations.

Even outside of a professional or medical context, listening is more useful than most people realize. It allows you to walk into situations and consider, "What do *they* want?" When you interact with people from that position, you listen to them and assess what they need from a genuine and giving place. It is the opposite of *using* someone else in a negative sense; that is, being opportunistic and taking advantage of other people for short-term gains without any interest in connecting with them, reciprocating, or building a relationship.

When you offer your skills or abilities in a genuine way, or put someone else's unique talents to use in a genuine and reciprocal way, it has a different bent to it than "using" someone just for a one-way transaction.

The ultimate win-wins in life and business are when no one is getting used. Instead, they are being "utilized." It's one of five methods Dan Sullivan lays out in his thinking tool he calls The Opportunity Filter®. According to Dan, we can be paid for our work in five distinct ways. Aside from being utilized, we can be rewarded, appreciated, referred, and enhanced.

As it turns out, all five ways also happen to be *useful*.

Domino: Being useful begins with being *caring*. It takes two parts: being aware of other people's needs, wants, pains, and problems, and then offering a solution. In doing so, be an active listener, empathize, and don't overwhelm, and give solutions that are simple to execute.

Questions for you: Do you practice both parts of being caring in your own relationships? How could you improve?

Being Grateful

When it comes to gratitude, I can't think of a more shining example than my late friend Sean Stephenson.

Sean was both one of my best friends and one of the funniest people I'd ever met. Due to a brittle-bone condition he was born with called osteogenesis imperfecta, he had broken more than 200 bones in his body before the age of 18 and was in a wheelchair.

From an early age, Sean was made fun of by other kids and had to learn very quickly how to deal with all that negativity and overcome it. At some point, he decided that he would take any negative attention he got and turn it into humor, caring, compassion, and an amazing speaking career.

If people were going to look at him anyway, he figured, he might as well be a public speaker. Though he never grew taller than three feet, Sean was an absolute giant when he was onstage.

Over his long career, he became a therapist, a hypnotherapist, and a doctor. He did an internship for Bill Clinton when Clinton was president, he spoke at schools, and he did a TED Talk from prison. He was on Jimmy Kimmel, he was on A&E in a television program called *3 Foot Giant*, and he wrote a book called *Get Off Your "But"* about how to put away your excuses to live a better life.

He had experienced about as much pain in his life as anybody I have ever known, but he always had a smile on his face. Even in the face of failures and disappointments, Sean had a line he would always say: "Rejection is God's protection." Even an atheist could understand the message. His go-to tools in any situation were fun and gratitude—all the way to the end of his life.

On August 28, 2019, Sean had a wheelchair accident at home and his wife, Mindie, rushed him to the hospital. Sean was texting me on the way there and FaceTimed me from the parking lot when he arrived. Meanwhile, I started rushing over to see if I could meet him before the doctors tried to do a final surgery on him to save his life.

Even in those serious circumstances, Sean was living his message all the way to the end. From his hospital bed, his last words were "This is happening *for* me, not to me."

In short, being grateful is a feeling of joy for life and for living. The more you are able to stay in *true* gratitude, the better you will be able to *respond* to life rather than *react* to it.

Expressing gratitude for life and for people around you is a valuable life skill, but it doesn't always come naturally; it takes serious practice. It is easy to feel ungrateful, to act entitled, or to always find fault, but that is a bad habit.

I've experienced so many ungrateful people firsthand—even after someone (sometimes me, sometimes friends of mine) had done tremendous things for them. The energy of entitlement or a lack of gratitude is a "taking" energy that doesn't give anything back. For that reason, takers tend to be ungrateful.

There's a hidden lesson in that as well. Givers tend to be very grateful—and what's interesting is that the more you give, the more your gratitude seems to grow.

If you volunteer at a homeless shelter or do any sort of volunteer work, you see what your giving does to the people receiving that energy. You learn the actual spiritual connection that your energy has to other people, and it builds your gratitude muscle. In fact, seeing it recharges you!

Moments like this show that gratitude goes both ways. You can give gratitude to the world, but you also want to receive it back as well so that you can keep expanding. After all, you can give a lot to the world, but if you don't let other people fill up your tank, you'll get depleted eventually.

> **Domino:** Being grateful is feeling *joy for life and for living*. Being in that state lets you respond to life rather than react to it — which in turn makes you more attractive and gives you a better energy. Because of this, givers tend to be grateful — and takers tend not to be.

> **Question for you:** In what area of your life would having more gratitude allow you to have more joy and more ability to respond to things rather than react to them?

Being Valuable

Value is a hard thing to quantify because it encompasses everything I've mentioned so far and more. It's also highly subjective. Whether real or perceived, value is in the eye of the beholder.

In a sense, value is that intangible X factor that certain people have. Sometimes it's a light in their eye, a unique wit, or their presence when they walk in a room.

For this principle, it's hard not to think of my late friend Dave Kekich.

Like so many special and high-value people, Dave had a unique view of life and a singular life experience that led him there. Early in his life, he became a millionaire and had all the external forms of what most people would consider wealth. He had a beautiful girlfriend, a Mercedes convertible, a house on the beach, a great career, and a great business. Then one day, after an accident at the gym, Dave became paralyzed.

After that, a lot more negative things happened to Dave very quickly. First his business partner stole most of his money from him. Then his girlfriend left him. Finally, he became permanently paralyzed from the waist down and lost his ability to walk.

His spinal injury occurred in the 1970s, and the technology didn't exist yet to fix his injuries. He was told he would have to spend the rest of his life in a wheelchair. In spite of that, he was still one of the most charming and charismatic men I ever knew—and he used that situation to fuel his drive, passion, and charisma even further.

After his injury, he reevaluated his entire belief system around life and death. Technology was getting better all the time, but by the time it could actually advance enough to fix his injuries, he figured, he would no longer be young enough to enjoy it anyway. With that in mind, he started wondering: What if there were ways to extend human life further than anyone thought possible?

Initially, Dave's questions sent him through years of raising money for paralysis research—but later, they took him in the daring new direction of life extension.

Dave formed a nonprofit devoted to life extension and looking for holistic and synergistic ways to extend the human life span. Although Dave "died" on September 9, 2021, at the age of 78, he is now cryonically suspended at Alcor in Scottsdale, Arizona. Maybe one day Dave will be back with us to fulfill the mission of #100 of his *Kekich Credos* (the full list of which is available on www.JoePolish.com/WIIFT):

> "The purpose of life is to delay, avoid, and eventually reverse death."

There's an old saying that goes, "If you want to sell what John Smith buys, you got to see through John Smith eyes." It's a way of articulating value: that which is valuable must be something that someone else actually *wants*.

In some ways, what is valuable is not necessarily "fair." It goes back to the notion of not being your own customer. Just because *you* respond to someone one way based on your background doesn't mean that everyone else will. We don't get to dictate what other people want and need.

In some circumstances, value can start from the same place as gratitude. It can begin with being caring and conscientious about what other people want; the difference, however, is that rather than *giving* them what they want, a valuable person *embodies* the essence of whatever those wants are.

That means, in another sense, value is more about self-worth and self-image than the other two principles are. Because the world is an enormous place and values are relative, it means that there is room for everyone to shine.

Another way to put it is that everyone has taste buds. If you are trying to sell filet mignon to a vegan, you are probably not going to get very far—no matter how good a salesperson you are. Similarly, you are likely not going to sell a plant-based, antioxidant-packed acai bowl to someone who only lives off fast food (though for the record, there are worse things in life than eating a bite of fast food every once in a while—and even acai bowls have their limits!).

In life, each one of us is a meal of some kind. Who is to say which is better, the filet or the health bowl? Both the bowl and the cut of meat are valuable, but whether that value is recognized or not can depend on the situation.

When I was younger and still in active drug addiction, there were times that I could've been close to dying because of my drug use and the dangerous situations I was putting myself in. During those times, when someone would show up to my house with drugs, there was no one in my world who I perceived to be more valuable at that moment.

In fact, from my addiction-induced point of view, drug dealers were *useful* and I was *grateful* when they came! They held so much power over my world and they were *valuable* to me—but as this situation illustrates all too well, what is truly valuable and what appears valuable is always up for debate.

As these examples show, all three principles of being useful, grateful, and valuable are important and we can (and should) embody them as much as possible, but the more nuanced truth is that all three are in constant tension with one another, and we can move back and forth between them in any given situation.

Think about it: How often is the most *grateful* person in the room also the most *valuable* person in the room or the most *useful*? How often is the most *useful* person the most *valuable*?

To be entirely blunt, gratitude goes a long way all the time . . . but it can go an even longer way when you're not very useful yet. If you don't have many skills or connections but you're eager to learn, optimistic, and energetic, you will start to generate energy and attention until your skills and network materialize around you.

If, however, you start acting overly grateful to be sitting at the negotiating table when you're at the peak of your powers, the reaction from the room is going to be significantly different.

Domino: Being valuable is often about self-worth and self-image — and is not necessarily fair. It can involve utility and gratitude, but it is also a quality in the eye of the beholder. A valuable person *embodies* qualities someone else wants to embody themselves, and this changes from situation to situation; this means everyone is not equally "valuable" to everyone else, nor is that necessarily a bad thing.

Question for you: At this point in your life, what do you find most valuable in other people, and what do you think most people find most valuable about you?

THE QUICK AND DIRTY GUIDE TO BEING MORE USEFUL, GRATEFUL, AND VALUABLE

It's easy to intellectualize every interaction we have with people, but at the bottom of it all, everybody is looking for love—it's just that sometimes we look for it in the wrong places.

The insight we should follow is if we know the wrong places, we should start looking in the *right* places, even if those places seem counterintuitive or we feel resistance in going there. Generally, the things we don't want to look at or the help we don't want to ask for is what we need the most.

As Joseph Campbell said, "The cave you fear to enter holds the treasure you seek."

Related to this idea of getting out of your comfort zone, or pushing into new areas so you can grow, is an idea that comes up again and again in life. People aren't just born useful, grateful, and valuable. They have to *work* to get that way.

You can't expect the qualities that would give you an amazing life to just fall in your lap—that would be entitlement, which is the opposite of gratitude. Instead, you have to seek out opportunities to hone those qualities by asking yourself questions. *How can I help here? What do I have to be grateful for right now? How can I offer more value to the world?*

Of course, when it comes to value, as we've seen, we have to differentiate what is real value and what is up for debate. For the mere fact of being alive and conscious, you have value. You are valuable because you are you and because you exist, and nothing can change that fact (though we find it all too easy to forget).

When we're talking about value here, it's built on top of that truth. That secondary value we're talking about is how you move through the world and how other people respond to you. It's not that other people's opinions of you don't matter at all, because they do to a degree—it's just that you can't stake your value on something that can go up and down every day. You have to stay anchored in your own goodwill and your own value. Then you have to put in the work so other people can see it too.

Many of us have likely been on the receiving end of other people's usefulness, gratitude, and value in our lives and felt how powerful it can be. When people we don't know show even a moment of gratitude or usefulness, it can improve our mood and make our day better—but when we connect with people who are almost *always* grateful, useful, or valuable, it can change our entire *lives*!

I call these people "first dominoes," because their impact can be so great that they set off chain reactions in our lives, causing many other "dominoes" to fall into place. Other first dominoes could be life-changing experiences we have or great ideas we get from a book, but more often than not, it's other people who are leading us into those big moments of insight.

While we might wish other people would come in our lives to be our first dominoes, the lesson that's easier to miss is that we can (and should) be first dominoes to other people. Doing so pushes us out of our comfort zones and actually makes it more likely that we'll meet more people who will be first dominoes for us as well.

The point is that these people and experiences don't just fall out of the sky most of the time. To find them or experience them, you have to put forth the effort and energy to create and generate them. To have people consider you valuable, you can't just sit around and expect things to happen to you or for you. You have to make them happen. If you wait around hoping to be discovered, you may be waiting your whole life.

As a simple example from my life, I've been sending personalized birthday videos to people for years. Doing it is easy, but it has created much better relationships, inspired some of my friends to do the same for others, and opened doors for me. If you go online and type in "Joe Polish Happy Birthday," you can see a few examples!

Imagine if you spent a year writing 5 to 10 personal notes, postcards, or cards every day acknowledging someone, thanking them, or sharing an article, video, or even a meme with them (with the caveat that they would *want* to receive these from you, of course). A year from now, your network would expand beyond your imagination, and you would be thought of as so much more caring, useful, valuable, and attentive than you are today!

This is one of my own, personal secret success recipes— and even though I've written it in this book, I still know that hardly anyone reading this book will do it. But if you do, it can transform your life and your business.

Becoming useful, grateful, and valuable isn't complicated—but nobody said it was easy, either.

Domino: To practice all three values, send messages to 5 to 10 people in your life every day showing appreciation, a sense of humor, or just saying hello. Few people will do this, but it has the power to change your life.

Question for you: If you made a commitment to send messages to people in your life, who would you most look forward to getting back in touch with?

KEEPING EVERYTHING IN BALANCE

I started writing this book before and during a sabbatical I took to recharge myself and my life so that I could come back with a new perspective. In that time, I've lost some very close friends, including Dave and Sean, whom I've written about here. As a result, my perspective on life has changed.

When you're in the moment, it's easy to judge people, to size people up, or to get caught up in comparisons—even when your relationships are going well. As soon as those people are gone, however, you would do anything just to have more time back, to have more mental space to focus on the good things you shared with them.

Before it's too late, it pays to realize that most people are trying to do the very best they can do, even when they're screwing up. This doesn't mean you should hang around people who are throwing grenades at you—in fact, you should get the hell away from those people. But it does mean that the more you can understand human nature, the more you can understand how *you also throw grenades*, and how you might learn to stop throwing them in the future. Once you understand that, you might be able to teach other people to put their own grenades down as well.

To practice, it helps to do what my friend Keith Cunningham calls "thinking time." Sit down and just ask yourself the question: "How can I be more useful, grateful, and valuable to my company, to my clients, to my community, and to my family?" Then ask, "How am I NOT being useful, grateful, valuable, and attentive to the same group of people?"

Investing just 10 or 15 minutes on those exact questions will lead to countless new ideas and opportunities to be a better person. Doing so will quickly make you more aware of where you are not being useful, grateful, and valuable, and where you could be more of those things to improve your life.

> **Domino:** It pays to realize that most people are trying to do the very best they can, even when they're screwing up. This doesn't mean you should tolerate bad behavior from people — just that understanding it can help you understand yourself as well.

> **Question for you:** In which of your relationships could you use more tolerance and patience — and which ones could use a little more distance?

The Dominoes:

- To connect in virtually any situation, focus on being **useful, grateful, or valuable**—or some combination of all three. Put another way, all three of these things deliver a *positive result* of some kind to other people.

- Being useful begins with being *caring*. It takes two parts: **being aware** of other people's needs, wants, pains, and problems, and then **offering a solution**. In doing so, be an active listener, empathize, and don't overwhelm, and give solutions that are simple to execute.

- Being grateful is feeling *joy for life and for living*. Being in that state lets you **respond** to life rather than **react** to it—which in turn makes you more attractive and gives you a better energy. Because of this, **givers tend to be grateful**—and takers tend not to be.

- Being valuable is often about **self-worth and self-image**—and is not necessarily fair. It can involve utility and gratitude, but it is also a quality in the eye of the beholder. A valuable person *embodies* qualities someone else wants to embody themselves, and this changes from situation to situation; this means everyone is not equally "valuable" to everyone else, nor is that necessarily a bad thing.

- To practice all three values, **send messages to 5 to 10 people in your life every day showing appreciation, a sense of humor, or just saying hello**. Few people will do this, but it has the power to change your life.

- It pays to realize that **most people are trying to do the very best they can, even when they're screwing up**. This doesn't mean you should tolerate bad behavior from people—just that understanding it can help you understand yourself as well.

Exercises and Action Steps

1. The Postcard Challenge

One of the best and simplest exercises that will massively increase anyone's network is also one that very few people will actually do:

Send 5 to 10 messages to people every day showing sincere appreciation, sharing valuable, funny, or useful things, or just acknowledging people who have helped you.

You can send them to your own staff, personal friends, prospects, or even people in the business world. You can also learn more about the postcard challenge on www.JoePolish.com/WIIFT.

2. The First Dominoes

As we mentioned before, the power and importance of a "first domino" that sets you on a better path can't be overstated. Finding these dominoes in our lives changes us and the people around us for the better.

Still, we don't often keep track of those dominoes with the people we meet or experiences we have.

A core component of my philosophy is to be a giver, and being a giver means recognizing and appreciating your first dominoes that put you on a positive or ELF trajectory in your life. Keeping those dominoes front of mind is the purpose of this exercise. It works like this:

1. **For the areas of health, wealth, and relation-ships, who was your first domino?** Rather than just listing the person for each of these characters, write the story of how you first met and your early experiences together in as much detail as you can.

2. **For the same areas, who have you been the first domino for?** Again, tell the full story rather than just listing a name. For this one, you may have been the domino for someone (or multiple people) in one area but not in others. Since this is a way of illustrating where you *give* the most to others in your life, take note of areas for improvement.

3. **Finally, what was the first person, book, idea, and event that put you on an ELF trajectory in all three areas?** Once again, write these down with some additional detail beyond just listing them—mention what about that thing impacted you or how you felt.

By doing this, you accomplish several things at once. First, you create a gratitude list of the people and things that have caused the greatest impact in your life. On its own, this can be a reminder to show appreciation for those things or to reconnect with people over that impact.

Second, part 3 of the exercise also serves as a cheat sheet of how *you* can pass the momentum of those first dominoes on to other people! If you've ever wondered how to give more value in a certain area, look at your list. If someone asks you about help, who could you introduce them to? What book could you give them?

Chapter 5

TREAT OTHERS AS ~~YOU~~ They LOVE TO BE TREATED

The best connections and relationships you make in life come down to the simplest things—and often, they have to do with being authentic and knowing how other people want to be treated.

This was what led to my first meeting with Sir Richard Branson.

It started when a friend called me up one day in 2006 and asked, "Hey, would you like to meet the billionaire Sir Richard Branson?"

"Okay," I replied. "What's the catch?" He explained he had a friend who was organizing a dinner with Richard but that it required a $5,000 minimum donation to his charitable foundation Virgin Unite. I thought it over for about 30 seconds before I decided I would donate triple the required donation.

I had made donations like that to foundations before—and of course, I wanted to meet Richard. The chance to meet and connect with him, I felt, would be worth more than the price of admission.

At the dinner, it was clear I wasn't the only one who'd had that idea. There were about a dozen people there doing whatever they could to get some time with Richard, but they were all asking him the most serious questions about climate change, business strategy, and so on.

The event was hosted by Mike Faith, the founder of Headsets.com, and Richard was being warm and kind to everyone, but I knew I had to talk about something else with him. *This is the guy who signed the Sex Pistols*, I thought. *He ran Virgin Records. He's hung out with musicians and rock stars and, jumped out of hot air balloons!* (This was all before he had gone to space with Virgin Galactic.)

We were all sitting at a long table preparing for dinner when I asked him, "Hey, what was it like to hang out with Sid Vicious and Johnny Rotten?" Right away, his eyes brightened.

Though we were all at the private dinner to raise money for charity, which was a serious affair, there was no reason why we couldn't have more fun in the middle of it. As we spoke more, Richard was taking a liking to me—and because of the questions I was asking, the tone of the conversation changed. Soon, Richard was asking everyone around him how old they were when they lost their virginity!

With everyone loosened up, the conversation turned toward Virgin Unite and what the organization stood for. The project was trying to unite entrepreneurs all around the world to work together toward positive causes, including one about supporting entrepreneurs in poorer countries, which was a mission I was completely aligned with.

As the night went on, I shared the experience I had using marketing to help raise awareness for charities, specifically by using education-based marketing. After hearing me speak, Richard was intrigued.

"Could you put this all into writing for me?" he asked at the end of the night, and gave me his e-mail.

After that evening, I made a sizable donation to Virgin Unite and paid Richard another fee to speak virtually at a livestream I was hosting the following year (another lesson in having conviction in your ideas and putting your money where your mouth is to make them happen).

After that, things moved quickly. Before long, I had interviewed the head of Richard's foundation and even had Richard speak at one of my Genius Network events. As our relationship deepened, I became the biggest fundraiser for Virgin Unite; helped them develop their business model, which they still use to this day and which has made them millions of dollars; and even earned some new insights about how many foundations aren't all they're cracked up to be (and how to run my own charitable foundations).

Still, none of it would've been possible if I hadn't treated Richard Branson the way *he* wanted to be treated. Though that can sometimes be the same as how *you* want to be treated, the difference in emphasis is crucial.

Domino: The best connections in life come from knowing how others want to be treated — and often the difference between success and failure is in the tiniest details.

Question for you: What techniques do you or can you use to learn more about how other people really want you to treat them rather than just assuming?

YOU ARE NOT YOUR OWN CUSTOMER

I've met many interesting people in the world of addiction recovery, one of whom was a female dominatrix.

She told me stories about men, some of them famous, who paid her—not for sex, but to be dominated. In her sessions with men who hired her, many wanted to be humiliated, verbally insulted, physically beaten, and other similar things.

As we spoke more, she explained that it was consensual and that the men enjoyed it, even if it could be emotionally and physically painful. She also revealed that the work was a way for her to process her own anger and resentment toward men that came out of her own background. And she told me she grappled with the possibility that she and her clients had sexual addictions—which raised questions about how much of their behavior was a therapeutic "choice" and how much of it was simply a compulsion that helped fill a need.

Either way, the point of this story is not to point fingers at what people like or don't like in their sex lives. It's to show that people are drawn toward different things and can match up in different ways, whether those ways make sense to you or not.

The bottom line is you can't always explain why people like the things they like. Another way of saying it is that you could write a whole novel explaining why someone likes what they like.

For the dominatrix I met, she'd had negative experiences with men throughout her life and in childhood that had shaped who she was as a person. As she grew up, those experiences influenced what she did for work and how she channeled that energy into other outlets.

I can only guess at her customers' motivations. Presumably they came from equally complex backgrounds that they were working out (in additional to craving the dopamine surge that often accompanies pain).

Here's another way you could think about it. The people who love country music will be able to appreciate many different registers of guitar twangs, vocal yelps, and sad lyrics. Someone who likes heavy metal won't hear any of that nuance—but they'll have a deep understanding of blast beats, heavy riffs, and how talented various screamers are.

In other words, what one person loves isn't the same as just anyone else, just like what you love isn't the same as what other people love.

It's the true meaning behind this axiom: *you are not your own customer.*

In life, you are always selling your ideas, interests, and passions to other people in order to connect with them—just like in business, you're selling a product or service in exchange for money or a customer acquisition. But in order to really do this, you have to understand the exchange from the *other* side.

What's in it for them? Getting a new connection might be great for you, but what would it do for the other person? What do they need that you can provide?

On a smaller level than making new connections or selling someone something, this is about learning how to talk and act around people to connect with them while still being genuine to yourself.

To do that, you have to discover what other people would love.

Domino: To connect with others, remember that you are not your own customer. What you like is not necessarily what other people like.

Question for you: Are there any situations in your life that you could solve more easily by thinking more about what the other people around you like?

LEARN WHAT OTHER PEOPLE LOVE BY SPEAKING THEIR LANGUAGE

Perhaps the easiest way to discover what people love is just to observe them and listen to them. What brings them joy? What are they interested in? What can they not stop talking about? What do they *complain* about?

There is a lot of wisdom in the idea that you are the sum of the five people you spend the most time with, but people sometimes take that too far when it comes to complaining. They say that anyone who complains is negative, and you can't have negative people around you if you want to be a positive, growth-oriented person, and so on.

I have a different perspective here. Sometimes, and with the right people, I love to complain!

Complaints are a way to get to know other people, just the same as anything else. They help you discover what causes them pain and how you might alleviate it by giving them something they want.

I was talking with Gary Chapman, the author of *The Five Love Languages*, after he gave a talk at a seminar some years back. He told me, "If you want to know someone's love language, listen to what they complain about."

That insight is true beyond romantic relationships—it can be just as powerful professionally. Complaints can be gifts, because what people complain about reflects what causes them pain.

Though Gary wrote his best-selling book all the way back in 1992, *The Five Love Languages* is still as relevant as it ever was to understanding relationships. In his model, he explains that in romantic relationships, there are five main ways that people want to give and receive love: through words of affirmation, quality time, giving gifts, doing acts of service, or physical touch.

In friendships and in the workplace, Gary's insight holds true as well even if the "languages" aren't the same (in fact, Gary even has a book specifically for workplace interactions).

Just for starters, you can find out what people care about by looking at their social media and doing some simple online searches. Beyond that, you can ask them questions. What books do they read? What movies are they interested in? Have they ever written articles? What are their hobbies?

The ironic thing is that people are often so fixated on showing their own value that they keep talking about themselves without asking other people questions or showing any curiosity.

One thing almost all people love is talking about things they are interested in.

Domino: People rarely tell you exactly how you should treat them, but to find out, learn about what they love. What brings them joy? What do they complain about? The skills for success here are curiosity and genuine interest in other people.

Question for you: What are the things that bring you joy and that irritate you, and how do they differ from some of your closest friends?

PEOPLE SKILLS ARE ALL ABOUT SITUATIONAL AWARENESS

When I interact with new people, I often start by trying to tell them jokes.

I'll start with less risky ones to gauge if they have what I consider "a real sense of humor" and if they like sarcasm. I deliver the jokes in a playful tone of voice—because it's not always what you say, but how you say it. That way, you can incrementally determine just how much other people like a certain kind of humor.

Feeling your way into interactions is all part of situational awareness, seeing how your tone and delivery is going over with specific people in a specific context. It's a lesson I learned the hard way in one of my very early interactions with Dan Sullivan.

Over the last 20 years, I've worked with Dan a lot in helping him grow Strategic Coach—but that opportunity almost slipped through my fingers because of my first day consulting with them in 1999.

At the beginning of our session, I met with Dan, his wife, Babs Smith (who ran the company), and one of their team members, Catherine. I was young, and because my expertise was marketing, I was confident about my own skills in the area and eager to show them off.

As a result, one of the first things I said in the meeting was, "Your marketing sucks." Little did I know that Catherine was the marketing director!

The rest of the meeting seemed to go well from my perspective, and I gave them all the best advice I had to give—but I had started things on the wrong foot.

Dan told me the next day that he was on board with my ideas and strategies, but I had to get the rest of the team on board too. He also told me I had pissed Babs off.

"There are two ways to influence people," Dan said. "You can tell them what's wrong and how to fix it; that's the first way. The second is to tell someone what's right and how to enhance it. You get very little resistance and way more buy-in. One approach says, 'Here's what's wrong with you.' The other says, 'Here's what's right with you.'"

It was an important lesson that I connected with immediately, and I learned something very important that day.

When I said, "Your marketing sucks," their team heard me insulting their hard work and their integrity. Because of that, they didn't want to listen to me or utilize the advice and strategies I was offering them. Although I later managed to become the top referrer of clients to Strategic Coach (and still am to this day), it took almost *five years* to fully repair the trust with Dan and Babs. It was a mistake I didn't want to make again.

(Fortunately, today, Dan considers me one of his best friends and has been a member of Genius Network/100K since 2010. He's also my top-referring client and we do a podcast together called *10xTalk*.)

Of course, even well-intentioned people make mistakes and put their foot in their mouth from time to time. It's a reality that has to be accepted, because that's what life is! Still, the story doesn't end with you making the mistake. Most mistakes are retrievable.

When things backfire in social situations, I'm always reminded of the word *responsibility*. The main definition has to do with what we owe one another, but I like to think of it in shorthand as "respond with ability."

A lot of people do not respond with ability when they screw up. They respond with negligence, or they make things worse. There's a saying I love that goes, *"The only thing worse than singing the wrong note is singing it louder."*

It's common sense, but people sing the wrong notes louder and louder in social situations all the time.

If you find yourself not connecting with someone or rubbing someone the wrong way, the first thing to do is *stop doing what you're doing.* After that, you can ask questions, identify your mistake, and then course correct. As the old saying goes, sometimes the best way to get out of a hole is to stop digging!

In the face of mistakes, remember: you are either winning or learning. Sometimes the biggest failure is the failure to get the lesson. The only way you get good at anything is by finding out what *doesn't* work.

> **Domino:** Deep relationships sometimes can't get formed without leaving the "comfort zone" — but you can't go too far out of others' zones too quickly. With new people, try to gently push boundaries to create real connections, but use situational awareness to know how much to push or prod.

> **Question for you:** How many relationships in your life could you deepen by pushing them slightly further out of the "comfort zone," and how would doing so enrich your life?

SITUATIONAL BEHAVIOR AND AUTHENTICITY

One of the fears people have in networking and social situations is how to be "authentic."

To a lot of people, being authentic means having an emotion and immediately sharing it in its raw form with whoever is around them. With that belief in your head, whenever you encounter a situation where someone makes you angry or disgusts you and you don't immediately unload on them, it creates dissonance.

Are you not being true to yourself by not shouting and calling that person an asshole? Can they tell you're holding back? Are you being "fake" by filtering yourself or by adjusting your reactions?

Let's take a step back here. First, the idea of "authenticity" that so many of us have bought into is a little faulty. If the idea behind being authentic is just "what you would do in a given situation," then anything you do in *any* situation is "authentic" simply because you did it!

Second, what we actually get hung up on is not our own inner sense of authenticity or identity (we usually have a good idea about that). We get uncomfortable when we know what our inner values and ethics are but we feel ourselves breaking them.

Another way to say that is that there is a *huge* difference between situational behavior and situational ethics. When it comes to building rapport, that translates to being very comfortable and fluid in your behavior, but firm in your ethics.

To better understand this, think of how great therapists work with clients who are dealing with trauma or topics that are difficult to talk about.

To a therapist, a client might say something like, "That asshole was so rude to me!" Without missing a beat, a great therapist might reply in a neutral, curious tone, "I see. What did that asshole do?"

Without overtly saying it, the therapist is showing the client that they hear their anger and understand their position, inviting them to continue. The real meaning is not conveyed by *what* they said but *how* they said it.

This is a form of mirroring, which is a well-known technique to make people comfortable and build rapport. In this case, the therapist keeps using their client's *language* without taking on their client's *beliefs*. In the process, they can nudge their client into new ways of thinking that could relieve the client's stress or make their life better.

But mirroring has broader implications than some people realize. In the interpersonal sphere, it shows up in the form of a concept I first learned in the world of sales and persuasion. The concept is: "Deal with people at the level at which they respond."

This means that when you're thinking about how to treat people to build rapport with them, you're allowed to be flexible. Even if you're polite and restrained in a professional context, you can loosen up when you're around your friends because those contexts are different and require different kinds of communication to build rapport. Even among friends, you can have some you talk politics with and others you don't. You can have some who are very sensitive and others you talk shit about without worrying about hurting their feelings. Just as different settings need different kinds of communication to build rapport, different people may also need different things from you. Still, even if you're playfully rude with one person and gentle to another, that doesn't make you inconsistent or inauthentic.

If anything, it might just mean that you're *consistently* considerate of the feelings of people around you.

You might have a way you would prefer to behave and communicate in all situations, but you're still allowed to change that or do things that might not come entirely naturally to you depending on what a situation needs. In fact, sometimes you might *have* to so that situations unfold in a way that suits your deeper intention—such as deciding *not* to flood a person you have a crush on with texts even though you want to (and even though you *would* like your crush to text *you* all the time), or *not* signaling that you have an amazing hand to the other players at a poker table (even though you *do* want the other players to signal their hands to *you*).

All of the above is why you can be a kind and caring person who is *also* a smart-ass who makes fun of their friends constantly, or a thoughtful potential romantic partner who is *also* cocky and aloof while flirting to get another person interested. What's wrapped around your behavior counts for *everything*. And like always, there is a lot to learn from sales on this subject.

Upon making a sale, a common mistake inexperienced salespeople make is *they keep selling*. The customer has already agreed to buy the product, and they're still listing ways that the product will improve their life. Don't do that!

In life as in sales, part of delivering value is in timing and dosage—as the saying goes, *"The difference between lettuce and garbage is timing."* When selling someone a product or doing a behavior you wouldn't normally do, the idea of a minimum effective dose is helpful: you want to do just enough to get the job done and no more.

After all, a teaspoon of honey in a cup of tea is delicious—but teaspoon after teaspoon after teaspoon when you're just trying to enjoy your cup ruins the entire experience.

Domino: Escape anxiety in social situations by remembering: everything you do is authentic because you did it. It is okay to change your situational behavior to mesh better with others — what causes problems is changing your *ethics* and the cognitive dissonance that causes.

Question for you: For behaviors that you think are inauthentic or inconsistent with who you are, which ones are actually at odds with your core beliefs and values and which ones are simply new or unfamiliar to you?

TREATMENT AND MISTREATMENT VS. NUTRITION AND TASTE

In considering how to treat others the way they would want to be treated, it presupposes that we not *mistreat* them. But what does that mean, exactly? What if you're a parent whose kid wants to eat ice cream every day for lunch?

Obviously, on a surface level, a kid might like to eat ice cream for almost every meal—but from a parental perspective, to allow this would actually be mistreatment rather than treatment. One way to think of this is that treatment and mistreatment can be likened to nutrition and taste. We might like the *taste* of ice cream more than the taste of broccoli, but broccoli is inarguably more nutritious, so a parent who makes their kid eat broccoli sometimes is treating them better than a parent who only gives their kid ice cream.

Of course, a kid is an unusual example, because parents are tasked with making many decisions for children that they might not make with other adults. To bring this fully into the adult realm, consider addiction.

As a person in recovery, I know firsthand that there are many addicts who would love to consume, partake in, or be given alcohol, cocaine, sex, gambling, food, sugar, and whatever other drug, substance, or behavior under the sun every day. But giving them those things would mean harming them.

Even so (and depending on the context), things aren't always so black and white. In some situations, it might be a "better bad decision" for a person with powerful sexual urges in a committed relationship to watch porn every now and then rather than drive to a strip club or start having affairs every time the desire strikes. This can be nuanced because adults are ultimately responsible for their own decisions, but the way to stay on the right side here is to stay on the side of your own ethics and character. If you know that treating someone a certain way would be causing them harm (even if they would seemingly respond "well" to it), don't do it. And if you feel you've lost control, seek help.

Part of this comes back to the concept of responsibility as our ability to respond to others, and what responsibility we truly have to other people. So, what is your ultimate responsibility? In part, your responsibility is to focus on the outcomes of your own actions.

The way most people often love to be treated is with dignity, respect, love, and care, but if you hire a personal trainer to train you, you don't want them to go easy on you. You want them to push you.

The same goes for therapy. Why do people sign up for it? Is it just so the therapist will tell them everything they say is right? It probably better serves them if they can find out where they are slipping, what's wrong, and how to improve. If someone wants growth, you serve them best by treating them with what they ultimately want.

My friend the late Sean Stephenson would explain how when there is a shipwreck, the Coast Guard attempts to save the people *swimming toward them*. In that situation, the Coast Guard wants to save as many lives as possible, but they have a limited amount of time and energy to do so, and they might not be able to save everyone. They can maximize how many people they save by helping the people who are coming at them, who are close, and who are helping to save themselves. This is important to understand as it relates to how you treat other people in your own life and who you invest in.

Spending resources on people who you know you can't reach, or who won't appreciate it or don't care, is probably not your best use of time and energy. Part of being a connector is to observe not just what someone says verbally, but what they swim toward versus what they swim away from, metaphorically speaking.

Domino: Treating others well versus mistreating them is like the difference between nutrition and personal taste. Parents know letting their kids eat only candy would be *mistreatment*, even if the kid "liked" it. Adults can make their own choices, but your responsibility is to focus on the outcomes of your own actions.

Question for you: In any part of your life where you feel you are spread too thin, who are the people in that area that are "swimming toward you" and how are you prioritizing them?

DEALING WITH "HATERS" AND NEGATIVITY

There's a famous saying: "You can't cheat an honest man."

The principle behind it is that if you have good character, you become harder to take advantage of, because you attract and associate with other people who have good character.

On one level, the principle is sound—it shows that being a good person and playing well with others is beneficial for you and for the world around you. But it needs to come with a warning.

No matter how good a person you are or how much integrity you have, you will encounter negative people who want to take from you. It happens to everyone, and it has happened to me.

A friend of mine introduced me to an individual who was interested in joining Genius Network. When I met him, he seemed like a high-achieving person who would fit in well.

Within Genius Network, there's a policy that if you're new and we don't know you, you have to join the $25K group first for a minimum of one year before advancing to our $100K group. There are multiple reasons for that. One is to make sure members get a ton of value for their business first before investing more and moving up to a higher level. Another is to familiarize them with all the concepts that we discuss and refine.

But the most nuanced reason is that spending time in the $25K group for at least a year allows me, my team, and all the Genius Network members a much deeper view into who someone really is.

In retrospect, it was a rule I should've heeded more closely.

In this case, the individual insisted that he start at the $100K group without going through the first level.

"I really want this!" he said. "I'm ready for it, I swear!" After some back-and-forth, we made an exception to our rule and let him in.

In Genius Network, the benefit of $100K is that you can also attend $25K meetings for no extra charge—so before long, I was seeing him at every single meeting we had to offer. Typically I encourage that, as it spreads more value and connection to both groups—only in this case, something seemed slightly off.

Sometime after, this person approached me to record a training program and a livestream he was doing and wanted to do it at my office. It was a little bit of a strange request since we didn't know each other that well, but it was clear he was committed to the group. Since he was a $100K member, I let him do it for free.

Then, as his first year of membership was nearing its end, this person decided to start complaining and shared that he was never included in the Genius Network's private Facebook group.

I was a little confused—it was clearly a minor administrative mistake and nothing more, because the Facebook group is an absolutely minuscule part of the membership. I was frustrated that he would imply otherwise and give my team a hard time. Still, we resolved the problem promptly since it was our honest mistake.

Unfortunately, he wasn't satisfied.

The Facebook group incident became a "hook" for him. He started using that tiny negative experience to corner me any moment he could and complain about things he had expected to receive from Genius Network that he thought he hadn't. Of course, throughout that time, he was still attending all of our meetings, doing interviews with other members, and making business deals!

Everything came to a head when he cornered me again after a Genius Network meeting and wanted to talk to me. My assistant, Eunice, and I spent an hour listening intently to his complaints and reservations about the group. Finally, he proposed a solution that would make him happy:

"I want to keep coming to $100K, but I'd actually like my wife to join with me as well, so I can pay for her yearly membership, but because of all this, it would be great to get a credit or something. So, I could pay $50K for her or so, and then get next year for free."

I was dumbfounded. He was essentially asking for a 75 percent discount over a forgotten Facebook group invite! I wasn't even angry; I was just fascinated by him and couldn't guess what he would say next.

Then, in the middle of our heated discussion, he said something revealing: "You know, I used to go to hotels and talk to the staff in a way that would always get me a free hotel room, but I don't do that anymore."

That was a side comment he made on the way to a different point. I looked at Eunice and something clicked in both of our brains.

It was clear I was dealing with someone who was used to manipulating people and was now trying to do the same thing to me. I thought to myself: *This is not the type of person I want in my life, and especially not in Genius Network's $100K group.*

As I learned the hard way, there are some games in life that you can only win by not playing.

Some people will try to guilt the shit out of you, and they will attempt to manipulate you, especially if they are narcissists, sociopaths, or psychopaths. There are plenty of desperate people running around, and you cannot live on this planet without running into them. If you are a giver, you will cross paths with them. As I get older and more experienced, I realize how true this is more and more every day. Still, knowing that this is the truth can be helpful as you move through life.

If you are true to yourself and you try to be a giver in the world rather than a taker, you are doing your part. If after all that you get into situations with people who drain you or take advantage of you, don't internalize it. Recognize it for what it is and get out as quickly as possible! I know this is easier said than done, but what alternative is there?

If you are an attractive person (in any sense), more people will want things from you. The more in-demand you are, the more requests you will have—and the more you will need strong boundaries to filter them.

In the beginning, being in demand can feel great. But when you run out of time and energy to serve all the requests you get, it can actually become very draining. Ask any celebrity, anyone who craved attention before they were famous, and many will tell you that they later became depressed, reclusive, or even suicidal. There is a real dark side to success and to overextending yourself.

In this arena, the best thing you can do is to seek progress rather than perfection, as they say in the 12-step world.

The skills you develop by being a giver cut both ways. Offering the world a lot of value can make you a lot of money, but it can also attract a lot of people who want to take it from you. They will simultaneously resent you and envy you while also begging you to give to their causes and help them pay their rent.

If you are the giver, you are the one who will be hit up all the time.

It is obviously so important to be kind, compassionate, and caring, but do not be a doormat. Learning that has been one of the hardest challenges I've had to deal with in my life.

I genuinely like helping people, but sometimes, those feelings have made me a target. It has led to people hanging around only when things are good and then not being there when things were bad.

Take it from me: as much as you have to develop kindness, you also have to develop your Spidey senses to identify people who are energy drainers, time vampires, fakers, con artists, and charlatans—just the same as if you work on your biceps at the gym, you also have to exercise the other muscles as well.

Ultimately, you want to be genuine, caring, and giving to connect with other people who are genuine, caring, and giving. You can do what you can to call people out on their bad behavior and give them a chance to improve, but you can't make them change. What you can do is keep your distance and stop sharing your life or business with them. In short, life is not just about connecting with people; it's about connecting with the *right* people and disconnecting from the *wrong* people.

After that, know that every relationship still needs work and maintenance. You still need to treat others the way *they* would love to be treated. You need to be curious about others, speak their language, and not put yourself at the center of everything all the time. But you can minimize your maintenance by starting with relationships that work.

In many ways, your relationships and your network are like a garden you have to cultivate. You have to find the plot, plant many seeds, and then be patient as things start to grow. As they do, you have to identify and pull out the weeds that threaten to drain the life out of everything else.

But for the plants that remain, you have to water them regularly. Take care of them as best you can, because nothing will bear more fruit.

Domino: Accept that if you are positive and giving, you will attract negativity and takers. This is a natural phenomenon in life and doesn't mean you should be discouraged — but you should be careful, as you advance, not to get taken advantage of.

Question for you: Is it more important to you to be a positive and giving person than it is to avoid negative experiences?

The Dominoes:

- The best connections in life come from **knowing how others want to be treated and what they actually respond to**—and often the difference between success and failure is in the tiniest details.

- To connect with others, remember that **you are not your own customer**. What you like is not necessarily what other people like.

- People rarely tell you exactly how you should treat them, but to find out, **learn about what they love**.

What brings them joy? What do they complain about? The skills for success here are **curiosity and genuine interest in other people**.

- Deep relationships sometimes can't get formed without leaving the "comfort zone"—but you can't go too far out of others' zones too quickly. With new people, try to gently evaluate their boundaries to create real connections, but use **situational awareness** to know how much to push or prod.

- Escape anxiety in social situations by remembering: **everything you do is authentic because you did it**. It is okay to change your situational behavior to mesh better with others—what causes problems is changing your *ethics* and the cognitive dissonance that it causes.

- Treating others well versus mistreating them is like the difference between nutrition and personal taste. Parents know letting their kids eat only candy would be *mistreatment*, even if the kid "liked" it. Adults can make their own choices, but your responsibility is **to focus on the outcomes of your own actions**.

- Accept that if you are positive and giving, **you will attract negativity and takers**. This is a natural phenomenon in life and doesn't mean you should be discouraged—but you should be careful, as you advance, not to get taken advantage of.

Exercises and Action Steps

1. What's Pissing Me Off?

Because relationships between people are like mirrors, treating others as they would love to be treated often starts with getting clear inside yourself first.

If we don't do any reflection or inner work, we sometimes carry around resentments and hurts that we think other people can't see (even though they end up affecting our behavior toward them).

Having those strong emotions isn't wrong, but stewing in them and letting them disconnect you from people is a problem. Fortunately, it's a problem that can be solved with *action*—and the first step is to identify what's bothering you.

That's what the What's Pissing Me Off? exercise is for. To do it, answer the following questions:

- **What's pissing you off?** Your answers can be very specific things related to behaviors your friends have had, or they can be more general things about the world around you or tendencies that you notice. Write them all down (around 10 things).

- **Why?** For each of the answers you gave, write an explanation for why that thing irritates you so much. The more you write and the more specific, the better.

- **How can you get back on track?** Once again, for all the things you mentioned, write down an

action that you could take that would help with
your irritation or resentment. Maybe you need
to have a tough conversation with a friend—or
maybe you just need to watch fewer hours of
TV news (or stop watching it completely).

The important part of this exercise is to identify any
emotions that are clogging you up inside and to get them
out with constructive action. Doing this will free up your
mind and your heart to open up to others and to the world
around you.

2. If I Could Have It the Way I Want It

After you've done the above, you'll have a good idea of
what irritates or frustrates you in life. The next thing is to
move beyond that sense of outrage into even *bigger* action.

In other words, you need to think of a plan to make
the world more like the better place you want it to be. To
do so, use the bigger, more abstract answers you listed
in the first exercise, and for each one, answer these
questions:

- **How is this thing now?** In as much detail as
  you can, write about what is causing this situation or problem. If it's a relationship, write
  about the roots of the dysfunction or disagreement. If it's something bigger, like "the government," narrow in on which part bothers you,
  how it works, and why it works the way it does.

- **How would it be if you could have it the way
  you wanted it?** As in the above, be as detailed
  as possible. What other outcomes would you

most want to see, and what process would those outcomes follow?

- **What ideas or connections could help make that vision become a reality?** Write two lists for this one. The first can be dedicated to the plans and ideas that might help, whereas the second one can be dedicated to the people who could carry them out.

- **What are the next action steps to make those ideas and connections happen?** For each set of ideas and connections you come up with, break them down into three steps—each with its own *what, who, and when. What* would need to be done? *Who* would do it? *By when* would that thing need to happen?

One of the hardest things in life isn't that we don't care about making big changes, it's that we can't see *how* to make them. As a result, situations seem so overwhelming that we slip into apathy and despair.

Part of reversing this pattern is to get clear on what we want and how we want to be treated. Once we do that, we can make a plan and put it into action. The important thing to remember is that you'll need to connect with other people to make big things happen—and understanding what they want from life and how they want to be treated is crucial to that.

Though there's no one answer for how to do that for others, using this exercise to understand yourself is a good place to start.

Chapter 6

AVOID FORMALITIES AND BE FUN AND MEMORABLE (NOT BORING)

If it isn't clear by now, a big part of my outlook on life has to do with being kind to other people and being grateful for what you have as much as possible. But with that said, it's hard for me to experience deep gratitude without fun, enjoyment, and humor in my life—and in the people around me.

Unfortunately, not everyone feels the same way I do.

I'm sensitive to the atmosphere around me as much as I can be, but my entire life, I've skewed toward twisted and slightly inappropriate (sometimes very inappropriate) humor. To me, it's just jokes, no matter what—though of course every situation and context is different.

Whenever I'm connecting with someone new, I view any relationship we might have as collaborative. I try to gauge how much energy I can put in or how far I can take a joke and then I look for what I get back. While the goal is never to be offensive or hurtful (though that can happen sometimes even despite best intentions), being humorous, fun, and interesting is an incredible way to build and keep rapport with other people.

And as we've already established, building that rapport is the first step to relationships with other people—and all the good things in life that follow from that.

WHAT ARE FORMALITIES?

Before going any deeper, it helps to know what we mean by formalities and what we don't mean. One person who framed the subject better than most is Robert Heinlein, the famous science-fiction writer, who wrote in the late 1970s:

> Moving parts in rubbing contact require lubrication to avoid excessive wear. Honorifics and formal politeness provide lubrication where people rub together. Often the very young, the untraveled, the naive, the unsophisticated deplore these formalities as "empty," "meaningless," or "dishonest," and scorn to use them. No matter how "pure" their motives, they thereby throw sand into machinery that does not work too well at best.

What's so smart about Heinlein's point is that it shows that formalities are not just something that can be done away with entirely. They have a very real purpose: making human interaction kinder, gentler, and generally easier! Still, I would argue that there is a difference between *formalities* in the strictest sense and *basic manners* in general.

What Heinlein was talking about certainly applies to manners, which are a fundamental way of treating others considerately and with respect. On the other hand, formalities—things like asking about the weather, using boilerplate greetings for everyone, always hiding your opinions and personality lest you offend someone—should be used very sparingly.

In my view, manners are in their own category; formalities are the polite things people feel like they *have* to do whether they want to do them or not. Often, they amount to "fake" behavior done out of obligation instead of genuine participation and collaboration with another human being.

When someone says, "Have a good day!" when you're having a bad day, it's an example of formalities failing us. Do you want to hear that from that person at that moment? Does that person have any reason to think you want to hear that? Do they even know you're having a bad day?

That doesn't mean it's not worthwhile to greet people. We have an 80-year-old Genius Network member named Joel Weldon, a Hall of Fame professional speaker who has been paid to speak at more than 3,000 events and coached well over 10,000 speakers. In fact, he's personally coached over 200 of our Genius Network members. Joel has a simple change he makes to that phrase: instead of saying, "Have a great day!" he says, "Make it a great day!"

As he puts it, he's not assuming you can automatically "have" a great day, he's inviting you to *make it* a great day. Granted, this still might not be what you want to hear when you're having a bad day, but it's a better version because it's genuine and actually shows that the person saying it wants to connect.

As I've experienced firsthand, when it comes to building rapport, excessive formalities can put up walls and boundaries when what you want to do is take the walls down. Life is about being relational, and being relational means dropping the fake nonsense.

Worth mentioning here as well is that you can still be professional and somewhat "formal" as the setting dictates without being fake—and while being fun. For example, if I go to a high-end restaurant or a business meeting where there is a dress code, I'll wear a suit or do whatever I need to do to adapt to that environment. But I always remember that *I'm* wearing the suit; the suit isn't wearing *me*.

> **Domino:** There is a big difference between formalities and basic manners. Manners and treating others well are almost always good — formalities are the forced versions of kindness that can often be inauthentic and bad for connection.

> **Question for you:** In what situations in your life have formalities made it more difficult to connect with other people?

USING SOCIAL CALIBRATION TO AMPLIFY THE FUN

Obviously, being yourself in different environments and with different people is a creative act, and there are nearly limitless choices. In every situation, you have to choose: How much should you stand out and draw attention to yourself and how much should you try to get along with others?

There's no one magic answer for all situations here, but there is a principle of social calibration that will help you in almost any situation. In short, social calibration is a lot like being aware of your environment, but specifically in the sense of interpersonal behavior. And there are many details that factor into it.

For example, if you're going to a business meeting or a networking event, is it the first time you're meeting these people? Is there anyone in the room who knows you or who has your back? Is anyone in the room particularly sensitive about any topics because of their background or anything else? Is there any topic that the people in the room particularly love talking about?

With new people and when making a first impression, you often have to be much more observant and "tightly calibrated" (so to speak) when considering what you'll say or won't say, or what jokes you'll try to make. Of course, as you make good impressions and build rapport, the trust deepens and the comfort zone widens, and you can start to loosen up.

Once you have a network around you with some close friends you trust, being fully yourself and not second-guessing your thoughts and opinions will ideally become second nature. Even so, sometimes you'll still have close friends who are sensitive about certain subjects and you'll respect their boundaries willingly also.

And sometimes you have close friends whom you can tease or perform for a little bit just to push them out of their comfort zone. It's something I've done before with many of my friends, but one of the more memorable times was with Dan Sullivan and his wife, Babs.

We were checking into a hotel room after an event and there was an attractive woman at the desk checking us in. At the time, I was single, and as we were checking in, I decided to joke around a bit.

"Listen," I told her, "first off, I want to let you know that I'm pretty tired and need to just go to my room tonight. I know you probably want my phone number or you want to ask me out, but I'd appreciate it if you wouldn't, because I don't think this is going to work for us." Dan and Babs aren't used to seeing scenes like the one I was putting on, so at first they couldn't believe it—but then they couldn't stop laughing!

The woman checking us in was smiling and then cracking up as well, and for the rest of our stay there, she always greeted me by name whenever she saw me in the lobby. Making that joke at that moment was risky, because if I did it the wrong way, I might've made the woman uncomfortable, or someone watching could've found it offensive. Still, I was able to make that joke without making anyone uncomfortable because I practice social calibration all the time, and I was able to read the situation the right way for everyone involved.

Though risky jokes like that can backfire (and I'm not advising anyone reading this to do exactly what I did), it paid off by making the trip that much more memorable and way more fun. I could tell more of the story, but to keep it short, just know the entire situation turned out really well. In fact, Dan still mentions it!

Over the years, I've always said that you can gauge the value of many relationships by how often you laugh with the other person. It's often the people who make us laugh the most that we spend the most time with—and those people often tend to be the most fun and memorable as well.

Of course, some of the best and most hilarious inspiration on how to be fun and memorable has come out of my relationship with my friend Dean Jackson.

Dean Jackson has been doing online marketing for years and years and is widely known as the inventor of the "squeeze page," which was also known as a "shy yes" page and later evolved into the "opt-in" page, where visitors were encouraged to enter their e-mail addresses.

We've known each other for more than 20 years and are both co-hosts of the *I Love Marketing* podcast, and our friendship was sealed one of the first times we did a major event together. There were about 450 people in the audience, and Paula Abdul was there, and at one point in the show, I asked Dean to pull out his wallet.

He did—and the wallet he pulled out was a pink Hello Kitty wallet. As he showed the audience, it got a few laughs. Naturally, I asked him, "Dean, why are you carrying around a wallet like that?"

Dean explained that he had once been gifted a wallet from Jeff Walker, another smart online marketer, that came from the movie *Pulp Fiction*. For those who haven't seen the movie or need a refresher, it's the wallet Samuel L. Jackson's character carries that is plain brown leather— but with the words "bad motherfucker" stamped into it. As Dean explained, the wallet was a cool gift and he liked carrying it around, but he noticed that he was starting to get some looks and make people uncomfortable when it came out.

Then one day, he walked into a store in Toronto and saw a pink Hello Kitty wallet and had an epiphany about what "bad motherfucker" really meant. As he told the audience at our event, "The wallet I was carrying *said* it, but the Hello Kitty wallet *demonstrated* it." Because of that, he decided to switch over to the Hello Kitty wallet full-time.

Before our event, Dean got me a Hello Kitty wallet too, so after our back-and-forth, I pulled mine out as well and showed it to the crowd.

I've found that wherever I go with the Hello Kitty wallet, I instantly get reactions and start conversations. I was so taken by the power of the wallet initially that I even started A/B testing it against other wallets to gauge response and see if any others would get the same reaction. Sure enough, none of them did. It was clear Dean was on to something with it, and it began to evolve into an inside joke between the two of us.

Soon, we were both buying pink Hello Kitty wallets in bulk and telling the story at marketing meetups about our thinking behind the wallet. After telling that story for years and years (and burning through dozens of Hello Kitty wallets), sure enough, we had countless other businessmen and marketers carrying around pink Hello Kitty wallets.

Today, the model that Dean and I carry doesn't seem to be available anywhere! I don't want to say we single-handedly created a trend there, but I'll let you draw your own conclusions.

Domino: To win rapport, connect with others, and have more fun, think about social calibration — particularly with new people. How comfortable are they in your presence? What would it take for them to be more comfortable?

Question for you: How do you practice social calibration in your life right now, and what steps could you take to improve that skill?

THE POWER OF LAUGHTER

My friendship with Dean and the laughs we've shared are largely the impetus behind the *I Love Marketing* podcast. From that alone, I've seen just how powerful laughter can be as a bonding mechanism—but laughter is even more complex and powerful than that.

Laughter may be a bonding mechanism, but it can also be an ostracizing mechanism: often, the people laughing one way versus the other are diametrically opposed on a given issue as well. For example, a gang of bullies laughing at another kid are bonding with one another through their laughter, but their laughter is ostracizing the kid who is being bullied.

Laughter is also a healing mechanism. After all, some of the hardest things in life can only be processed by making jokes about them. For example, when people are ill, it's been shown that raising their spirits with comedy, jokes, and fun can boost their recovery. I believe laughter has a greater impact on a person's well-being than gratitude or grit, even though those are also enormously valuable.

No matter the specifics, the point is that laughter creates bonds—so it's important to understand it and to use it carefully.

The ability to read and understand people is important, because it helps you see the edge and build rapport quickly. I can be in a super-professional meeting, but if I talk about one of my frailties and make fun of it, or if I bust on someone because I've read our rapport correctly, suddenly the ice is broken and our connection is strengthened.

It's also true that sometimes that sense of humor isn't something you have to constantly be *doing*. It can be a more passive thing that keeps generating laughs, like the pink Hello Kitty wallet. Sometimes it can extend to an entire building.

One of the things we constantly hear from people who visit our Genius Network headquarters is "I love your building! There's so much crazy, funny stuff around here!" Our sense of humor at the building comes out of defying what people think is a "professional" work setting, and visitors take notice!

When people walk into my office building and into Genius Network, they see funny scenes, weird statues, and crazy art. This is because I want my environment to reflect what's funny to me.

I never laugh more than at my Genius Network events. Whenever I'm there, I'm constantly bantering with the other members. As all the Genius Network members have learned firsthand, when you are laughing, you are paying attention to another person. You are caring for them and caring about their reaction.

That exchange creates joy, and it makes people bond. When people bond, amazing things can happen.

But while it's clear that humor and laughter can do great things for relationships, not everyone feels naturally funny or comfortable acting that way. Because of that, I always tell people that if they want to be funnier, they should learn to make humor a habit.

We all have habits. They can be winning habits or losing habits. They can be million-dollar habits, health habits, and spiritual habits. Truthfully, none of us have any "bad" habits—we are just very good at habits that produce bad results. It boils down to the fact that "certain actions done in a certain way produce certain results," as my friend and Stanford professor BJ Fogg wrote in his book *Tiny Habits*.

So if you accept that premise, take a look at how consistent you are with things that create good results.

When I do addiction-recovery work, I can't work at my best if I don't put humor and fun into it. It's heavy work. There are people in the world who do heavy work; they don't have the freedom to be funny or be around funny people. I'm lucky that I do.

I could write an entire book on all the little nuances of how humor and rapport interact, but the point is that in many contexts, it's helpful if you can be funny. And if you want to learn to be funny, my best advice is to take an improv class. I always tell people to go to improv class (and some I even tell to go to clown school—seriously, it works). I've taken my own employees to improv because there are so many benefits to it!

One idea to make humor a habit is to start by identifying what *you* are really about and what you value. Once you know that, you'll have a better idea about what you find funny in the first place.

The reason to do this is because it's a precursor to *riffing*, which is a sure-fire antidote to being boring. It works so well that I even made my own list of "Joe's riffs," and I've been using them for years.

My list of "Joe's riffs" is filled with all kinds of different marketing concepts—and these are particularly valuable for seminars and speaking engagements. I've gotten so experienced with the concepts over the years that I can pick out a handful of concepts, apply them to the crowd I'm talking to, and I'll have a presentation.

This idea of riffs has come from needing to be prepared for speaking engagements at a moment's notice. It's helpful because I like every talk I give to feel spontaneous and "new" rather than overly rehearsed. A lot of professional speakers have a "signature talk" that they can do again and again, but not me. I don't want to memorize anything, and I'm also quite distractible, so I've given up on trying to stick to the same talk. I can speak to concepts, but I can't bring myself to say the same things over and over again, which is why I like riffs. By using riffs, I can draw on topics I'm confident in, but they always come across in a new way.

The funny thing about marketing techniques and exercises like this, by the way, is they can apply in virtually every area of life. You can even use them to help you pick potential partners or mates (as we discussed earlier in the exercise based on Annie Lalla's personal ad for a soul mate)!

Finally, riffs and everything else aside, it helps to have just a few jokes or lines that you can lean on in times of need. No matter how charismatic or interesting you naturally are, these can come in handy all the time.

The first time I interviewed Sir Richard Branson in front of 750 people at one of my Piranha Marketing events, I said to him, "If you and Al Gore were to get into a physical fight, do you think you could take him?" I asked him this live, and, of course, he stuttered a little bit because it threw him off guard, but then he totally cracked up laughing, and the audience did too. I said the same thing to Bill Clinton the second time I met him and got the same reaction.

Domino: Few things are as powerful as laughter when it comes to social bonds. Even if you don't consider yourself naturally funny, you can practice making humor a habit.

Question for you: Who is the funniest person you know in your life, what do they do that makes you laugh so much, and what can you learn from it?

BE MEMORABLE — AND ALWAYS IN A POSITIVE WAY

No matter what you're doing, trying to be memorable makes life more enjoyable. More pointedly, it also helps you get things done. No matter what you're trying to accomplish, the person who stands out is often the most likely to be remembered and called back.

Of course, how "memorable" you need to be depends on the context, and you only want to be as memorable as you need to in order to accomplish your goals.

You might want to be memorable just for an afternoon if you run into a server who is having a bad day and you want to help them feel better by telling them a joke or thanking them in a personal way. On the other hand, if you're trying to close a big deal, maybe you want to be memorable by sending more than a standard thank-you note and going further with a personalized gift.

The point is that it always helps to be memorable in a positive way, but what most people don't realize is they're always making impressions. People are always remembering us in some way—it's just not always positive.

Sometimes people get remembered as complainers, pains in the butt, or short-tempered. All of those people are definitely being memorable, but in a way that creates a negative impression and leaves them disconnected.

For marketing and business, I've created a concept I call the Happy Client Experience. I use it so much, in fact, that it's one of my riffs! In the riff, I explain that there are three types of experiences a client can have: they can get *less* than they expect, *exactly* what they expect, or *more* than they expect from an experience. Getting less means the client is *unhappy*, getting exactly what they signed up for means they're *satisfied*, and getting more means they're actually *happy*.

In other words, by striving to do the best you can and by going above and beyond, you can actually have a *happy* client. And even though the people you meet in your real life aren't buying services from you, necessarily, the principle is the same.

In any given situation, we have an expectation of how polite people will be, how kind they'll be, and how interesting the overall event will be. Similarly, we can get our energy drained by a disappointing social experience—or we can be invigorated when people surprise us by being kinder, cooler, and more memorable than we expect! The goal is to exceed whatever expectations someone has. That makes them happy and you memorable.

> **Domino:** You are always making impressions on people, so by default, you are always being "memorable"—the important thing is to be memorable in a *good* way rather than a bad one.

> **Question for you:** What first impression do you usually make on people, and what kind of first impression would you like to make?

BORING AND BEYOND

As a person in recovery, part of my life was constantly pursuing stimulation.

I have a creative brain and I like activity. I'm very curious about all kinds of things, and I find myself going down new rabbit holes and following brand-new ideas all the time. Because of that, I used to have an inner belief that I would repeat in my mind all the time like a mantra: *How can someone ever get bored? There are so many books to read, songs to listen to, things to do and experience!*

What I've realized later in life, though, is that needing to be constantly stimulated isn't necessarily a great thing all the time. The more constantly engaged you are in activity, the more you set up a rhythm of *needing* nonstop activity. It makes me think of a quote from Albert Einstein (which, incidentally, he wrote on a piece of hotel stationery in 1922 that later sold at an auction for $1.56 million). He wrote:

> A calm and modest life brings more happiness than the pursuit of success combined with constant restlessness.

There's wisdom in that quote—but it's also challenging, because when it comes to boredom, addicts become pleasure-deaf. This is true for addiction to drugs, work, or sex, and it's also true for all the areas of our lives that addiction is creeping into as I'm writing this. With the pandemic, constant propaganda, and so many other toxic forces, addiction is at its highest levels in human history.

If you're *constantly* on your phone, constantly on social media or *constantly* playing video games, or *constantly* consuming drugs, you're not allowing your body or spirit to rest. You're not in a parasympathetic (or, more simply put, relaxed) state, and the result is that you're burning yourself out. You're constantly seeking dopamine, but not in healthy ways.

You're likely losing sleep and becoming more anxious. You're more prone to eating crappy food, less likely to have the energy to exercise, and more likely to rely on other means of stimulation.

Once you get caught in this cycle, you keep looking for the next hit of excitement and you lose track of the bigger purpose. Depending how deep in you are, you may even be at risk of losing everything, including your life.

If you think about people in your life who are in this sort of state, they are *not* fun to be around. They might be memorable, true, but usually not in a positive way. Another thing to notice is that when you get into a self-destructive cycle, it's not just that it's unpredictable and dangerous for other people; after a while, it starts to get boring, for you and for others.

When it comes to being boring, the truth is, you are only boring to the degree that you can't evoke interest from other people. It means that as with everything else I've said so far, being memorable and fun also comes down to how much you can be concerned, caring, or actually useful to others.

First, you have to ask yourself: *Are they going to help me? Am I going to help them? Is this relationship going to help me? Is it going to help them? Is this person or relationship going to expand me? Is it going to expand them?*

Second, if you feel yourself getting into one of these negative spirals, it can help to take a moment to evaluate yourself.

Ask yourself:

"How much of my internal dialogue is filled with fun, with a sense of humor, with finding comedy in the pain?"

Then ask yourself:

"How much of my inner dialogue is filled with negativity, insecurity, or anger?"

By becoming aware of your inner dialogue, you can make efforts to shift it in a more positive direction and live a more fun and open life.

When it comes to other people, almost every human being has a fascinating story behind them if you know how to engage with them. If they are unwilling to engage, and you practically need to be a Houdini to pull anything out of them, then you may be better off walking away. All the same things apply to yourself as well. When you look at yourself and your life in the right light, you'll see fascinating things that you appreciate and want to share with other people. Of course, if you're unable or unwilling to do that, it shouldn't be a big surprise if people start to disengage from you.

Without having a good relationship with ourselves first, it becomes very hard to offer it to other people. It can take work, but a good first step no matter where you are is to follow these guidelines of being fun and memorable rather than uptight and boring—and if everything else fails, there's always clown school!

Domino: Being "boring" in social situations just means you are not evoking others' interest. Evoking others' interest is about what impact you can have on them, and being kind, cool, and interested in others often works well for this.

Question for you: What do you stand to gain by making it a priority in your life to be more interesting and engaging to others?

The Dominoes:

- There is a **big difference between formalities and basic manners**. Manners and treating others well are almost always good—**formalities are the forced versions of kindness** that can often be inauthentic and bad for connection.

- To win rapport, connect with others, and have more fun, think about **social calibration**—particularly with new people. How comfortable are they in your presence? What would it take for them to be more comfortable?

- Few things are as powerful as laughter when it comes to social bonds. Even if you don't consider yourself naturally funny, you can practice making humor a habit.

- You are always making impressions on people, so by default, you are always being "memorable"—the important thing is to be memorable in a *good* way rather than a bad one.

- Being "boring" in social situations just means you are not evoking others' interest. **Evoking others' interest is about what impact you can have on them**, and being kind, cool, or interested in others works well for this.

Exercises and Action Steps

1. Make Your Own List of Riffs

Just like I made my own list of "riffs" to generate conversation topics, you can do the same thing yourself:

1. **To start, take out a sheet of paper and do a brainstorm of all your core interests, values, and ideas.** Most of what we talk about should be authentic to who we are and what we're interested in, and it should draw on impactful stories or quotes that resonate with and help illustrate our points. This is the foundation from which all funny and interesting things spring.

2. **After that, make further lists stemming from those interests, values, and ideas that include the things you like to talk about most.** These might be things you love, things you hate, or personal stories/experiences you have related to each one.

3. **Once you have that, make even more specific lists for each of *those* topics.** In theory, you can keep this list-within-lists technique going for more and more specifics, but usually this step is a good place to stop. By now, you're getting away from general ideas and down to very specific applications and subjects that only *you* can speak to.

Even if it sounds a little unusual, the point is not to have a script that you recite the same way to everyone you meet. The point is to prime yourself with things to talk about and to have them in the front of your mind so they're more accessible. You can do this same exercise for both personal and professional conversation starters!

2. Take an Improv Class

If humor and spontaneity don't come naturally to you, the good news is these are things that can be practiced and learned. One of the best ways is to have funny friends and ask them about their senses of humor.

If all your friends are boring (kidding!), another great way to enhance your capacity for humor is to take an improv class. I'm entirely serious—there are few things that will loosen you up more than a good comedy class.

In real life, it's easy to get stuck in your head thinking about what you should say next, what the cleverest line would be in a given situation, and so on, but getting caught in that space disconnects you from other people. In improv, you don't have the option of getting caught there—you have to say whatever comes into your head *now*. If you don't, the scene falls apart.

If you feel like you want to take a class, don't overthink it. Just look up the closest comedy club, go there, and check it out. The point is not to become a professional comedian or learn how to be funny the "right" way, it's just to start making humor a habit.

This may seem like an intense challenge, but trust me, nothing will expand your comfort zone faster—and hopefully, you'll have some fun in the process.

Chapter 7

APPRECIATE PEOPLE

When the iPhone first came out in 2007, it made a huge splash. Before it, phones were mostly just phones—and the smartphones that did exist were clunky and not too impressive.

The iPhone was different. It was the smartest phone on the market and it was also the easiest to use. It was like carrying a desktop computer around in your pocket, and it was going to revolutionize how everyone communicated with one another.

The day they came out, I bought one at the Apple Store and the way I communicated with people changed almost as quickly. Before the iPhone, I had spent a lot of time calling people because I liked the personal connection, but when I couldn't make a voice call, I was limited to text-based e-mails and SMS messages. With the iPhone, I was suddenly sending people pictures and emojis and so much more (videos wouldn't come until a few models later). Soon I was sending audio snippets as text messages along with slightly inappropriate jokes, complaints, compliments, on and on.

Over the years, it has evolved into kind of a signature style of communication for me—and in the process, I have gotten thousands of people to send their first audio and video messages.

When it comes to the people who are close to me, I am in constant contact—and it often isn't goal-oriented. Some days I wake up and send close friends audios checking in about what is going on that day and occasionally videos of myself making healthy waffles (check out www. GeniusWaffles.com) or getting into a cold plunge.

Sometimes, I put people in group messages who don't know each other well yet and send them useful ideas, articles, videos, or podcasts (my own or other people's) to make an introduction. Other times, I text and leave voice notes to people to tell them what's on my mind, or about things I've read recently.

You might think this is something that I limit to my very close friends, but you'd be wrong. Maybe it started out that way, but over the years, I've expanded it to encompass many of the people I deal with. The number one way I communicate with my team is using audio and video messages.

The secret to it is that the people who get that kind of treatment from me are the people I *appreciate*, or who serve some useful purpose in my life or the lives of others I know. The funny thing is that as I get older, there are more and more people whom I appreciate—and the simple act of sharing so much of my life with them makes that appreciation grow even more!

It seems strange to write this down as if it's a tactic, because it's not—it's just a form of communication that helps me get a lot of stuff done that is so much quicker and more effective than sending text messages. Still, it's interesting to see the effect it has. Even if not everyone is used to being treated that way, almost everyone enjoys it or appreciates it.

It shows that I think enough of them to not think they're disposable. It shows that I think of them as real human beings and that our relationship can be as deep as we want it to be. It works for me and it works for them.

It bonds us together, and all of it happens because of mutual usefulness and appreciation. Even if my strategy isn't the one that everyone uses, it highlights an important lesson: in life, it is so important to appreciate other people.

LEARNING THE MEANING OF TRUE APPRECIATION

Ever since I was very young, I understood the power of being kind and curious about others. Appreciation for other people played a part in this, but I didn't fully understand what that concept meant until my early carpet-cleaning days.

When I was first starting out, the first major lesson I learned about appreciation came from a guy named Wayne who managed a janitorial supply store.

I was a dead-broke carpet cleaner living off credit cards and I had a new client on the hook who wanted me to clean their sofa. As strange as it sounds now, I knew exactly how to clean carpets—but cleaning a sofa the right way was a new challenge.

After doing a little research, it looked like I would need to buy a hand tool to clean the sofa, which would cost somewhere between $250 and $300 for the tool. At the time, whenever I went to the supply store, I could afford to buy a $20 jug of cleaning solution *at most*—and I was often doing it on a credit card rather than paying cash. Now I had to figure out how to get a tool I had no way of affording!

The day I went in, I asked Wayne at the counter if I could rent one of their hand tools since I didn't have the money to buy one.

"Just take it, dude," Wayne said, waving my concern away like it was nothing. "After you do enough jobs and you make a little money, then you can come back and pay me for it; how about that?"

I was in awe, but he wasn't finished! "The same goes for chemicals!" he said. "If you need something, just let me know and take whatever you need. Build up your business first and then come pay me back later." I was absolutely ecstatic.

With my borrowed tools and supplies, I was able to complete that first job and get more and more jobs, earning enough to pay Wayne back. Soon, my business was growing and within a couple years I 5x'd my business and eventually started selling marketing courses to cleaners— and as soon as I came out with my educational marketing guides, things skyrocketed for me.

But even as my business grew and grew, I would still go back to the same store to buy all my supplies—even if it meant driving 45 minutes across town from Chandler to Scottsdale to do it.

The second lesson I learned came from a guy named Ernie, who was a member of the Arizona chapter of the Carpet and FabriCare Institute. It was an organization for carpet cleaners in Arizona; they were looking for a new volunteer director for Arizona, and part of that job was to bring in some educational classes for the members who were professional carpet and upholstery cleaners and for people who did fire and flood restoration.

Of course, it was a role that most people already trying to run a business didn't really want to take; it was unpaid and seemed like it would be thankless, with lots of errand running and organizational work. But I saw it a little differently. I volunteered to become the director because I thought of it as a service position. I knew it would give me a reason to be around people in the industry who had been in the business a lot longer than I had, and there was so much I could learn from them.

As a result, I got in a position to organize events and put people together whom I wouldn't have been able to meet otherwise. One of those people was Lisa Wagner, who was very helpful in my business Piranha Marketing.

Later, I had a big job cleaning a very nice hotel with expensive Berber wool carpet that I just couldn't seem to get as clean as I wanted. It was a big deal to do the job right, so I knew I needed to ask for help. So I called Ernie.

Keep in mind that this person was running one of the top restoration companies in Phoenix at the time—it was literally a multimillion-dollar company! Even so, he came out and helped guide me on how to clean this type of Berber wool carpet.

When it was over, I was begging him to let me pay him for the help, but he wouldn't take my money.

"Don't worry about it," he said. "I'm just happy to help you." As a result, I ended up doing the exact same thing with him as I did with Wayne.

Later, I became the most well-known person in the cleaning industry. I appeared on the cover of several trade magazines including *Cleanfax*, the largest trade magazine for carpet cleaners in the world at the time—and just a few years before, I hadn't even known how to clean a carpet!

At any rate, as more business was coming to me, I started referring restoration work to Ernie's company, who helped me. It was the least I could do to show my appreciation.

The craziest thing about my carpet-cleaning journey is that I went from not being able to afford anything and using borrowed supplies to becoming a successful carpet cleaner and the top marketing advisor to the entire industry—and a lot of it was made possible by people like Wayne, Ernie, and Lisa!

> **Domino:** Appreciation pays compounding interest — both in personal relationships and in business.

> **Questions for you:** For the most impactful relationships in your own life, how has appreciation played a role in each one? How could adding appreciation in other relationships make them even stronger?

WHAT APPRECIATION MEANS TO ME

Appreciating people means being internally grateful and externally expressive so people are aware they are valuable and appreciated. Part of this means recognizing and being aware of a person's value or of a situation worth appreciating—and then raising the value of it.

When you tell one of your team members, a person providing you some type of service, even someone holding the door open for you, that you appreciate them, what you're really saying is you value them. You're saying that you respect them and you're thanking them for their help.

Appreciation is a simple concept, but it can be executed in so many ways. Aside from my unique messaging style, I have so many different appreciation practices that I work into my daily routine.

For starters, I show appreciation by making connections and sharing my knowledge and my ideas about business, addiction recovery, exercise and health, and books to read. I cannot tell you how many books I give away to people—not only my own books, but other people's books.

When I talk about appreciation, I'm coming at it from the idea of being a caring, valuable person, because that leads to others becoming more caring, compassionate, and conscientious. Of course, for this to work the way it ought to, that appreciation has to be *genuine*. Doling out undeserved appreciation just to appear caring and nice— or, even worse, to manipulate people—is just silly. It's only going to deplete you and create false expectations in others.

At the end of the day, you can fake appreciation, play politics, and flatter people, and you may still get a result— but it usually comes with diminishing returns. Next time, you have to do a *bigger* favor or you have to give a *better* compliment to stay in someone's good graces.

If not, you may just feel like you're out of alignment with your values because you don't *actually* think or feel the way you're telling others that you do about them. Over time, it will drain your energy—or you'll get found out and your relationships will hurt for it.

On the other hand, you can skip all those headaches by just being genuine. While I definitely operate in a way that tries to get me the results I want (and you should too), I do it in a genuine way by making sure the other person is getting what *they* want as well.

An easy way to think of it is with the book's title question: **What's in it for them?**

The point of asking that is not to make everything transactional but to guard against being manipulative or one-sided in your own actions. When you're interacting with other people, are you thinking about what they want and need? Are you trying to be helpful to them? Do you appreciate what they bring to the table and are you paying it back?

Another way of thinking of appreciation comes from my friend Ray Kurzweil. For anyone who doesn't know, Ray is an inventor and a futurist and has been a director at Google since 2012. He's received 21 honorary doctorates and honors from three U.S. presidents and has been called one of the most fascinating entrepreneurs in the United States. One of Ray's biggest ideas is the idea of "the singularity," when there will be a melding of humans and machines. In fact, we're already experiencing this with smartphones, VR, and other technologies that he refers to as "brain extenders."

While Ray's ideas appear to be mostly about technology and brain extension, you can think of the network effects of appreciation in exactly the same way.

Phones, computers, VR, and tablets expand our capabilities to find things out, to connect with others, to appear smart, to get answers. If you become a brain extender for others, people will love you the way they love their phones. If you think of yourself as an extender of what people want, they're going to want to hang out with you.

You do this by connecting them to people, insights, solutions, results, and so on that extend their capabilities, or simply by making them laugh or helping them get what they want. By doing so, everyone you touch sees their value increase; you are quite literally *appreciating* them.

Domino: True appreciation is being internally grateful for *and* externally expressive to others. In a literal sense, this "appreciates" the value of the people you show that energy to.

Question for you: How do you currently show appreciation for the most important relationships in your life, and how does doing so make them more valuable?

A $300 MILLION JOURNEY THROUGH INTIMIDATION AND APPRECIATION

Though mutual appreciation is a great thing to aim for in business and relationships, it doesn't always happen immediately for all kinds of reasons—and when mutual appreciation *does* happen, it doesn't always look like sunshine and rainbows. On the way to true appreciation, and often in the middle of it, there can be a lot of conflict to navigate.

One major roadblock to appreciation is intimidation, and it's not always clear how to deal with it. You can't truly appreciate anyone who intimidates you so much that you can't get close to them. Likewise, those people probably can't appreciate you because they don't respect you. In many situations, intimidation tactics might be better thought of as rapport tests.

That dynamic is one of the main topics in one of my favorite books, *Winning through Intimidation* by Robert Ringer, which was written in 1973. Though the title makes it sound like it's about learning how to win by intimidating others, it's actually the exact opposite—it shows you how to win *through* other people's intimidation tactics by standing your ground and not letting them derail you.

For as much as I talk about being kind and helpful in this book, intimidation is not always a bad tactic to use against people who are trying to intimidate you. Other times, intimidation can be a test that you have to pass. Once you do, you can make friends with people who will be brutally honest with you and push you forward by being allowed to play a little rough. Having people like that in your life can help you advance further and faster than you would otherwise as long as you trust them. Still, if you act like a doormat around those people, you'll never earn their respect, and you'll never get to that level with them.

My advice is this: Give people the benefit of the doubt, and rather than trying to judge every behavior you see, try to engage with people at the level they want to engage at instead. If they are kind and thoughtful, give them that same respect. If they want to compete or complain, engage them the same way if you want to!

Of course, if you're dealing with sharks who only want to hurt or take advantage of you, you may need to use an even harsher playbook or not engage with them at all. Still, in a lot of situations, intimidation is just a knee-jerk reaction or a test rather than a real threat—and people will *appreciate* you seeing through it for what it really is. For as much as we talk about being more thoughtful as a way to appreciate others, sometimes appreciation requires you to *stop* being so sensitive, get in there, and fight!

The connection between overcoming intimidation and appreciation may seem a little abstract at first until you experience it for yourself. I learned that lesson in my life after meeting Bill Phillips.

Bill Phillips is an entrepreneur and author, and when I met him in late 1995, his goal was to build the largest sports supplement company in the world. I was at a conference in Vegas that he was putting on and decided to approach him and show some appreciation.

"Hey," I said, "I think the magazine you publish and the advice on nutrition and exercise you put out to people is awesome! And your sales copy is phenomenal!" He loved the compliment and asked me if I wrote copy. I told him that I did, though I usually hired copywriters.

After that, he gave me his fax number and asked me to fax him some examples (after all, this was 1995). I first sent him some examples of my work, explaining my approach and giving some context. After some friendly back-and-forth with him, I sent him a quote for $3,850 a day for consulting services if he wanted to work with me, adding that I could come out in person to do so.

Shortly after, I got a letter sent via fax back from Bill that was two pages long. As I read it, it looked like my compliment wasn't going to result in new business after all, because he was not pleased with my offer. One of the lines Bill wrote kept echoing in my head:

> *I paid $11 million in taxes last year, why would I pay you $4,000 a day to tell me how to run my company? I have people waiting in line to write copy for me for free!*

It struck me as odd—if his time was really as valuable as he said, why would he spend so much of it writing me a long and insulting letter? That gave me an insight, and I started typing another letter to him in response:

If you have people lining up to write copy for you for free, they're obviously not very good at marketing themselves. You don't go to McDonald's and say, "Give me a Big Mac because I'm Bill Phillips and I'm rich. If I like your hamburger, I will pay you for it, but if I don't like it, then it's no skin off my teeth because I have restaurants lined up all over town that want my business because I'm so high and mighty." They would tell you to get lost!

I ended up writing about four pages in response before faxing it over to him. Soon after, he faxed me the same letter back with a handwritten response in the margins:

You're feisty! I like that. I'll be in touch.

A few days later, Bill overnighted a check to me with a first-class ticket to fly to Denver to see his headquarters in Golden, Colorado, and officially hired me to do some consulting for him.

On our first day working together, I gave him an idea for a multi-sequence mailing using an existing sales letter he had that was already working, and that idea later made him $6.5 million. We kept working together and in our early conversations, he brought up a new movie he had put together called *Body of Work*. It had cost him about a million to produce, but he wasn't sure about how he should distribute it.

Bill wanted to give away *Body of Work* for free, but he also didn't want to devalue the movie by doing so. I had just sent out a letter to my own marketing clients offering to send them a free interview with Gary Halbert on cassette, and I'd had the same problem Bill did: I wanted to give the interview to my audience for free because it contained so much valuable information, but I also didn't want them to undervalue it since they weren't paying for it.

To get around that, I sent all my clients a letter explaining my thinking and said that if they sent my office a check for $20 to the Phoenix Children's Hospital, then I would send them the cassette. I figured that attaching a price to the interview would make everyone value it more, and having any money I collected go to charity meant that the interview would still be a gift. Since that strategy had worked well to raise donations for the Phoenix Children's Hospital, I figured it would work for Bill as well.

After we discussed it, he ran an ad in his magazine *Muscle Media* (which had hundreds of thousands of subscribers) saying that he wanted to raise $100,000 for the Make-a-Wish Foundation. Without getting too detailed about the logistics, the idea was entirely based on reciprocity. He would send a free copy of *Body of Work* on VHS to any of his subscribers purely as a gift. In return, all Bill was asking was that anyone who got a copy of his movie would make a donation to Make-a-Wish. (Back then, there was no YouTube and no streaming video—people were barely even using e-mail for marketing!)

I was instrumental in helping Bill tell his story, position himself, and develop the advertising for the rollout. Initially, his community of fans had been mostly limited to bodybuilders, which was fairly niche. But as *Body of Work* circulated and Bill's business grew, he became known more broadly as a fitness expert (and as a generous person, as a result of his fundraising for the Make-a-Wish Foundation). The strategy was a major success, and it worked wonders for getting his sports supplement company a lot of exposure and getting his magazine to a much wider mainstream audience.

Bill's success and now-elevated stature led to a book deal for *Body for Life*, which he got a $500,000 advance for—an amount that was practically unheard of for a first-time author! I helped him add self-development concepts to the book and came up with many ideas for using *Body for Life* physique transformation challenges to market it (which more than a million people participated in).

Thousands of companies of all sizes started using the model I helped Bill develop—even the founders of Beachbody, which grew to over a billion-dollar brand, told me how much this model influenced their business. As a matter of fact, at an event I was doing in 2010 with Richard Branson, I introduced Bill Phillips and the founders of Beachbody, and they told Bill themselves how much our work had impacted their business. To this day, the seeds that Bill and I planted have grown so much that I'm not even sure how to measure their impact—whether financial, health-related, or otherwise!

Even so, all that value might not have existed without that first compliment—as well as the shit-talking faxes Bill and I sent back and forth that followed. As a result of our mutual willingness to stand our ground and argue things out, we formed an impactful connection—one that led to more than a million people improving their fitness through *Body for Life* challenges, made Bill wealthier, spawned thousands of similar businesses, and raised millions for charities in the process.

All the positive things discussed in previous chapters are forms of investment and appreciation, but what doesn't get mentioned as much is all the conflict and disagreement that gets folded into those endeavors over the years. In the long view, overcoming intimidation to form stronger connections with people and seeing your way through disagreements isn't in opposition to appreciation—it's actually a necessary *part* of appreciation.

Though Bill and I had ups and downs in our relationship, the track record we built together helped his company and led to countless people seeking me out for marketing advice. Even though I never got a degree in health or studied nutrition or exercise at a university, I've been involved with so many different people in the health and fitness industry—so much so that a large percentage of my clientele in Genius Network are medical doctors, naturopaths, chiropractors, people in the nutrition field, and mental health practitioners from psychologists to psychiatrists.

On top of that, the work I've done has led to me reading over 1,000 books, attending many events, and spending thousands of hours immersed in things related to health and fitness. And if I look at the thread that has allowed me to develop all of these relationships, it's aligned with a few simple strategies: seeing through intimidation and appreciating people.

> **Domino:** Appreciating other people is an *action* and must be done continuously—and sometimes it can only happen by overcoming intimidation.

> **Questions for you:** Where is intimidation stopping you in your own life? How could you stand your ground against intimidation to build more appreciative relationships?

HOW (AND WHY) PEOPLE GO UNAPPRECIATED

One of the most common reasons people go unappreciated is because they give everything they have away for free *to the wrong people*. Some people don't effectively establish authority, perspective, and value, so they get taken advantage of or taken for granted. Some people are simply too accessible and too available.

I don't necessarily exclude myself from that statement, either—the only reason I know any of these things is because I had to experience them firsthand, in multiple different ways that were so painful and left me so disillusioned. There are plenty of times that I've been targeted or manipulated by takers despite my best intentions.

When I decided to take a sabbatical in 2021, a lot of people who were used to having access to me all the time started contacting my office, e-mailing or texting me and my assistant, and showing up in my messages (even though they knew I was taking time away) saying, "I miss you!" or "Can I help you in some way?"

I appreciated some of those messages, but some others I got were trying to rope me into commitments or people who hadn't spoken with me in a while who were trying to get favors from me before I disappeared. With those, I realized an uncomfortable truth: those people didn't really appreciate me or respect what I was trying to do for myself.

Another common way people go unappreciated is when people find themselves under the thumb of manipulators. I have constantly seen kind, caring people be abused this way—and I've seen narcissistic, sociopathic manipulators get everything they want. It's hard to swallow, but it's a real dynamic that happens in life. I recently did an interview with Dr. Ramani Durvasula, author of the book *Don't You Know Who I Am?*, about how to deal with narcissists. You can watch the interview at www.JoePolish.com/WIIFT.

I have fallen into the trap of not being respected or appreciated myself, mostly because I made myself too available or I selected the wrong people to show appreciation to, even though I was coming from a good place.

But I've also had people who were shaking and nervous in my presence after they saw a talk I gave at an event. These are people who put me on a pedestal and think I'm a special human being because I've written books, I've helped people make money, I know famous people, and so on. That might seem better than being under appreciated, but really, it's not.

On one level, that kind of reaction shows that they think the other person has a lot of value, and sometimes that's all it is—but on another level, sometimes it means they don't view you as a real person like they are. The result is that some people who seem like huge fans are actually dismissive and not caring about your feelings!

Avoiding these traps becomes quite important as you get more successful, but the truth is it's helpful at any stage. While it's important to show others appreciation, it's also important to screen the people around you and to only give your energy and appreciation to the people who deserve it. And, while I love it when others show appreciation for others (it's something I constantly do), I am amused by some people who utilize appreciating other people as a way to link themselves to those people for self-serving purposes. On the one hand, it can be seen as thoughtful to acknowledge someone. But when the acknowledgment is attached to a sales pitch or used to get someone to read your silly social media post, I call this tactic giving "credit to credentialize."

One way I determine who becomes a closer friend of mind is by observing how they treat people who are less powerful than they are. If people are nice to me because I can do something for them, but they are not nice or are unreasonable to my team members, I fire them. I've also fired clients who were incredibly nice to me when I saw they were being rude to my team.

I know a company that would fly job candidates in for interviews and send a driver to pick the candidate up. The same driver would return the candidate to the airport after a day of interviews. What the candidate never knew was that the driver was part of the hiring committee. How that candidate treated a "mere" driver revealed a lot about the candidate's character, which the company weighed heavily in hiring decisions.

After I got burned enough times, these tactics start to make more and more sense.

> **Domino:** Being unappreciated or underappreciated can come from either giving someone bad energy or being manipulated by someone else's bad energy.

> **Question for you:** For the places in your life where you feel unappreciated, is it a result of something that you're responsible for or have you been manipulated?

APPRECIATE YOURSELF

There is another area of life where people go unappreciated—and it's a tricky one.

There are times in our lives where we are generous, caring, and full of life, and others when we are depressed, angry, and in a reactive rather than responsive state. The issue is that when you fall into a negative version of yourself, for whatever reason that is, it becomes a lot harder to show appreciation or receive it.

The lesson here is simple: you need to appreciate yourself first if you are going to spread more appreciation throughout the world. And part of self-appreciation comes from learning to stop chasing other people's validation when we're already doing everything as best as we can.

There are certain people who won't appreciate us or respect us, no matter what, and it has nothing to do with our actions. It's different if you have a good friend who starts distancing themselves from you because you've been thoughtless or cruel to them; those are situations that should be mended whenever possible.

On the other hand, sometimes people move into your life because they recognize your value and they want to take it without giving back. They do so because they think you will keep giving it to them forever—and because they think you won't ever say no because you crave their approval. These people are nonreciprocal, entitled, disrespectful, and often abusive.

In those situations, the juice ain't worth the squeeze. The amount of trickery and positioning required to change how those people view you is simply not worth it, because they're already showing you they're not people worth knowing. As the old saying goes, the best way to get out of a hole is to quit digging it.

There are certain people and situations worth cutting off. If you're working for a company and your boss is a raging abusive jerk, leave. If you're in an abusive marriage, leave. Sometimes this advice can even apply to your family. Why should you put up with your family's bad behavior if it's completely toxic?

I acknowledge that some people can't easily leave—maybe they have children or maybe they have financial and legal obligations they can't easily get out of. This isn't universal advice for every complex situation; all I'm saying is, the more you can take care of yourself, the more you can take care of other people—and the less torture you have to endure from others.

> **Domino:** To appreciate others, you have to appreciate yourself—particularly as you become more successful. This means being kind to yourself, but it also means setting boundaries, respecting your own time, and cutting off toxicity when necessary.

> **Questions for you:** Do you appreciate others as much as you appreciate yourself? In what ways does setting good boundaries result in greater appreciation?

WE ARE ALWAYS AFFECTING ONE ANOTHER

I've always said that a huge portion of what goes on in life—socially, psychologically, you name it—is mostly invisible to the naked eye. This is true for many things, but it may be the truest when it comes to appreciation.

In an ideal world, we would all walk around as our best selves, always being happy and satisfied and grateful to everyone we meet. Of course, as we've already said, that's not how real life works. Sometimes we have bad or terrible days, and sometimes we go into negative spirals that affect how much energy we have for other people.

Without even focusing on worst-case scenarios, what about the mental state so many people often find themselves in—a state of indifference and apathy? For a lot of people in the world a lot of the time, they're not euphoric or despondent. They're just doing what they have to do to get by, not looking forward to anything in particular and not thinking very far beyond that exact moment.

I'm saying this not to talk down on those people, because everyone can become complacent in their life no matter what level of success they have. It's easy to stop appreciating what you already have, and it's easy to become jaded and cynical when things don't go your way or life turns out differently than you thought it would.

All I'm saying is that we have to accept all that emotional volatility as part of life, and we have to practice gratitude anyway for the simple fact that we are always affecting each other whether we mean to or not.

Choosing not to be as respectful as you could be to someone you run into in life isn't actually a choice *not to do* something, it is a choice *to do* something else: to be mean or thoughtless or generally not live up to who you want to be.

The tricky thing about appreciation is that everyone around you has their own mental list of people whose approval they prioritize and who they want to appreciate them, and everyone's list is different. Often, people keep those mental lists a secret—but if you observe their behavior toward you and others, you can usually figure out whose opinions they really prioritize.

That knowledge is powerful because it can be so easy to manipulate for your own ends. On the other hand, that knowledge can also be a huge catalyst for making the world a better place.

If you see someone who really needs more appreciation and they're looking for it from people who aren't giving it to them, give it to them yourself! Show them what they're worth and watch them blossom into who they should be—and then watch as they repay it to you and to others.

How you talk, the tone of voice and gestures you use, and little things some people may not notice—these things affect everything all the time.

In saying this, I'm not saying you should be able to read everyone's mind and perfectly know how to appreciate everyone all the time. I'm saying that you can genuinely appreciate people at the intersection of their wants and your awareness of those wants.

Sometimes you do that with a smile, sometimes you do it with a kind ear, and sometimes you do it by selling them a product or connecting them to someone you know.

With appreciation, it's not about what you want. It's about what they want and your ability to link them to it. It's about what power they have to be helpful and valuable in the world and the space you can create for them to step into that power.

Domino: Appreciation has a bad rap as something naive or gentle. In reality, it's a very serious thing—and it can change lives in an instant.

Question for you: If you could only show more appreciation in one relationship or one area of your life, where would doing so be the most impactful?

The Dominoes:

- **Appreciation pays compounding interest—** both in personal relationships and in business.

- True appreciation is being **internally grateful for** *and* **externally expressive to others**. In a literal sense, this "appreciates" the value of the people you show that energy to.

- Appreciating other people is an *action* and must be done continuously.

- **To appreciate others, you have to appreciate yourself**—particularly as you become more successful. This means being kind to yourself, but it also means setting boundaries, respecting your own time, and cutting off toxicity when necessary.

- Appreciation has a bad rap as something naive or gentle. In reality, it's a very serious thing—and it can change lives in an instant.

Exercises and Action Steps

1. Write Your Appreciation List

Appreciation is easy enough to grasp, but it's sometimes harder to practice in the moment. Fortunately, there are ways to practice.

There's an exercise I've done with well over one thousand very high-level entrepreneurs who are millionaires. Though it's a longer process, you can do the short version of it quite easily:

1. **Write down the names of the most important people in your life, including who they are and what value they bring.**

2. After that, write down how often you see those people or how often you tell those people what they mean to you.

The exercise is short and sweet, but it's illuminating. What do you think the most common response to it is? You guessed it: that we're not focusing enough of our precious time on the people we care most about—and in many cases, we're not even telling them or *showing* them that they mean so much to us.

2. Appreciation Letters

After you've identified the most important people in your life, another thing I love to do is **write them a sincere letter**. This isn't the same as a short postcard or a text— both of those things are still great for connecting, having fun, and building rapport, but the point of this exercise is slightly deeper.

A handwritten letter says a lot, because it takes a lot of intentional time and effort. In the letter, explain to the person you're writing how you feel about them, why you appreciate them, and the impact they've had on your life— even better is if you can relate your letter to a problem that person is going through that they're trying to solve.

You can do this exercise with different people in all the important areas of your life.

If every day you sent out 10 thoughtful and intentional letters, e-mails, postcards, audio notes, text messages, or videos, and if you did that five days a week for an entire year—your network and the karmic value you would have earned through it would be enormous.

Chapter 8

GIVE VALUE ON THE SPOT

A decade ago, for one of Genius Network's $25K meetings, I reached out to Paul Zane Pilzer, one of the world's top economists and a former advisor to the Reagan administration, to speak.

To set up the meeting, I talked with Paul on the phone for about 30 minutes while running through how everything would go. We were going to turn off the video cameras and then do a wild Q&A session covering 10 things about the economy people don't know.

We had it all planned for a few weeks out, but the energy of the call and of that moment was too much to let slip. Paul was a guy who was very much in demand, and still is. He has been on the cover of hundreds of magazines, he's been in *The Wall Street Journal*, and everything in between. A lot of people don't know him as a household name if they're not into economics, but suffice it to say, he was a very important person without a lot of time.

But even with a plan in place, anything could happen in a few weeks. So I decided to jump on the opportunity.

"Let's do a quick interview as a teaser of what you're going to talk about," I said. "We can send it out to the people coming to the meeting and thinking of coming to the meeting, just so they're aware."

Without missing a beat, Paul agreed that it was a good idea—so right away, I called Dean Jackson for help recording it on the spot. After a few minutes, we had an audio setup in place and Paul and I started talking, and the teaser was just as good as I knew it would be.

A lot of the principles in this book have to do with mindset and the way you carry yourself in different situations. While that's all valuable in itself, all of that preparation doesn't mean anything without the right execution. There are a lot of ways to come up with value, but you have to actually *deliver* it for it to be worth anything. And that's what this principle is all about. To be most effective, you have to give value not in the future or in some abstract way. Instead, and whenever possible, you have to give it *on the spot*.

VALUE AND THE POWER OF URGENCY

One of the most important things when it comes to value is how "real" that value is. It doesn't matter if you know plenty of influential or useful people if you're not actually *doing* things with them.

In those cases, you're never offering anyone any help, and they're not offering you any aid either.

To understand this better, you can think of it outside of a business context. Think of a time when you've been out in the world and you've bumped into an acquaintance or a friend you fell out of touch with. What happens next?

Inevitably, someone says, "It's so nice to see you!" and then someone else says "We should get lunch sometime," or "We should work on something together soon," or something else vague and indeterminate. But how many times do those plans actually come together? Even more importantly, how many times do people even *want* to follow through on those plans?

In the rare instances when both people actually do want to get together or reconnect, my question is simple: Why not now? If it's so important, why can't we get coffee right now? Why can't we outline our collaboration right now? In a social setting, this kind of thing is already annoying enough, but in a professional setting, it's even worse.

While networking or at a conference, you'll often meet someone and start to make a connection, or hear something like, "Oh, so-and-so could really benefit from knowing you," or "These people could do a business deal together." But again, after that, e-mails or numbers get exchanged and follow-ups are promised but never materialize.

For me, whenever I'm in a situation like that and someone expresses some sort of pain, need, or opportunity, I scan the Rolodex in my brain and think of who I know. Then, instead of saying I will e-mail both people later, I text, send an audio or video message, or even call that person on the phone right then and there. I know there are some situations you need to think about more, and you can't (nor should you) act spontaneously every time. However, whenever you have a chance to "make the boat go faster" in real time, I recommend you do it.

That doesn't mean that you shouldn't send another e-mail later on as a follow-up, but that's not the point. The point is, if you're right there, do it right then! Make it happen! Don't fall into "paralysis by analysis" either by not making a decision or by keeping an open loop you don't want to keep open. This way you won't waste your time or the time of others, and you'll be able to squeeze the most value you can out of situations when they present themselves.

It reminds me of the "two-minute rule" I learned from my friend and productivity consultant David Allen 20 years ago. We spent a day together when I was helping him with his marketing and he was helping me with his GTD (getting-things-done) method. His rule was simple: if you have something to do and it would take less than two minutes to do it, just do it!

Yes, there are certain things that need to germinate. Many things take more than two minutes to do or to decide on. Sometimes ideas need time to dwell in someone's brain before they're ready to be shared. But saying "let's do lunch" just to be polite and not meaning it is a social tic and obligation you should avoid.

If you're wondering about how exactly to create value on the spot for people, author Robert Collier said that you should "enter the conversation already occurring in the prospect's mind." It's a keen insight into both interpersonal relationships and marketing.

If you study marketing, you tend to become a student of human behavior. Once you care about what somebody wants, you learn about that person's interests and who they are. Part of it goes back to the idea of being useful, grateful, and valuable. You can have countless relationships and opportunities in your life, but without taking the necessary steps to push those things into action, they won't help you.

In every situation, the first step is to ask yourself: *What is the thing this person wants or needs?* After that, the solution is literally to take action.

> **Domino:** Value depends on urgency. If you know many high-status or influential people but neither of you does anything to help the other, that value is not real.

> **Questions for you:** In your personal and business relationships, how often do you take action to turn potential value into actual value? What strategies could you put in place to do so more often?

DECONSTRUCTING SOCIAL MEDIA FOR MORE VALUE

Ever since marketing, networking, and business were invented, people have been flaking out on following through on plans, meeting up, or connecting people they said they would (the modern-day versions of this include canceling on getting coffee or forgetting to set a follow-up Zoom call). This much is obvious. What isn't as obvious is how much of an effect social media has had in this area.

Before everything was on the Internet, sales and marketing depended hugely on knowing everything there was to know about the people you were selling to. To that aim, old-school marketers once dedicated a lot of time to developing systems to learn that important information.

Of course, the gold standard in this category was originated by my friend Harvey Mackay.

Harvey is the author of *Swim with the Sharks without Being Eaten Alive*, along with six other *New York Times* best-selling books. Part of his *Swim with the Sharks* book was a seminal system called the Mackay 66, which revolutionized marketing when it first came out.

In short, the Mackay 66 is a customer questionnaire with 66 different questions on it to help salespeople understand who they are selling to. The questionnaire asks about customers' general demographic information, but also about their college backgrounds, how they feel about those backgrounds, their religion, and how ethical of a person they are (and how they feel about *that*).

The quiz gave salespeople very thorough information about a customer that went beyond simple numbers. Instead, it produced a complete psychological profile that salespeople could use to connect with their prospects. It humanized the sales process.

Though plenty of marketers built on top of Harvey's system and came up with their own versions (or just stole his without crediting him), what gets talked about less is how much social media algorithms have done all the same work for us.

Today, the biggest social media platforms are collecting data and metadata from us every second of every day—sometimes we feel like their algorithms know us better than we know ourselves! Although marketers can find ways to use their platforms, they are often damaging when it comes to really *seeing* people or connecting in person. (And when it comes to violations of privacy and the manipulation of news and world events, social media can be downright dangerous.)

Social media makes everything overly convenient. Now when we go online and look at people's profiles, we get everything about them in one place at a moment's notice—but a side effect of that is we think *we* did the work getting to know them anyway, except all we did was look at a page and then stereotype them!

The downsides here are obvious: We become less curious, we get pushed more into our heads, and we make assumptions about people that stop us from connecting in real life. As a result, we also fail to deliver value to them in person and on the spot.

This is where an old-fashioned tool like the Mackay 66 can be more powerful than anything AI, machine learning, or algorithms can provide. Those advancements in computation seem like they allow everyone to know everything, but though they may provide content, they don't provide context. Sometimes, doing an exercise like the Mackay 66 the old-fashioned way helps you internalize that information in a way that automation doesn't.

The funny thing is, before you meet someone, you can look at their social media profiles . . . and then use the questionnaire on the profile, if you want. Based on what an algorithm is showing you (and what the person is choosing to show), what can you ascertain about that person? If they constantly post pictures of fancy things, or try to inspire other people to be jealous, or just post pictures of themselves, what does it say about them? What does it say if they are constantly picking fights with people online?

This exercise doesn't tell you everything, but it helps you become curious again, which helps you get past simple thoughts and stereotypes. Then, with a more thoughtful approach to background research, you now have a list of *real* questions you can use when you meet in person, which makes you curious all over again.

To put it simply, being curious makes you open to others, and being open to others lets you see what they want and need. Finally, seeing what people want and need lets you *deliver value* to them.

In marketing, the quickest path to the sale is to identify a person's current want and combine that with intelligent relationship building to present them an enticing and irresistible offer. In connecting with other people when you're not selling them anything, the process is essentially the same.

When it comes to delivering value, the biggest takeaway is to look for the quickest path to the value. If you become known as a person who takes action urgently and thoughtfully, you will immediately be seen as valuable—and that value will only compound as you help others.

That's Genius Networking in action: giving value on the spot.

Domino: Delivering value requires learning about other people. Social media has automated this process, although enabling connection in ways that were previously not possible can also make us detached. To change that, we have to relearn or develop these skills and be curious about people again.

Questions for you: What information about other people do you rely on social media for that you take for granted? How could you internalize that information better or make that knowledge more intentional?

SPEED OF IMPLEMENTATION AND THE FIVE-SECOND RULE

It's obvious enough that if you are in conversation with someone about a business idea and you say, "Let's continue this conversation tomorrow," your chances of putting together a deal are much greater than if you say, "Let's continue this conversation in two weeks."

In business and social situations, it's easy to get sucked into paralysis by analysis. We wonder who knows whom, what might be appropriate to say, how forward we should be, and so on—when in reality, we usually have a lot more permission to make small mistakes and push forward than we realize we do.

If you don't say the perfect thing or someone says no to you about an on-the-spot follow-up, it won't be the end of the world. In fact, nothing bad will happen at all. You might not get what you want, but you will get more information that will save you time in the future.

The point is that even if many entrepreneurs and high-performing people lean toward perfectionism, it's often better to be punctual and prolific rather than perfect in most cases.

In other words:

Do your best to not take life so seriously, because most situations don't require it.

In some cases, it's obviously better to really think things through before taking action. If you're a fighter pilot or a surgeon, for example, precision means the difference between life and death.

But social events and business mixers are rarely life-and-death situations. There's usually not going to be major fallout from taking action, so it's best to increase your *speed of implementation*. That's a term Eben Pagan uses to talk about acting swiftly and with a sense of urgency— basically, getting off your ass and taking action before you talk yourself out of it.

Even if that sounds easier said than done, particularly for people who have a lot of anxiety or who are easily distractible, there are exercises you can use to get out of your own head. One of them that I use a lot comes from author Mel Robbins.

Mel teaches what she calls the five-second rule (do an online search to learn all about it). The general idea behind it is that if you have a desire to act on a goal and don't act within five seconds, your brain basically kills it.

This might sound like a lot of pressure. Fortunately, you can use this information to your advantage.

Whenever you feel a desire to act, the rule, according to Mel, is to count backward from five. Then, once you hit "one," you *have* to take action. It's a simple method for actually kicking your speed of implementation up a gear.

Doing that will increase your chances for success, because you'll be taking more action and getting out of a "stuck" mindset.

What Mel's advice says to me is that if you're not getting ahead in life or developing relationships, it might be because you're hitting the snooze button too much. You might be letting your doubt and anxiety get the best of you.

Instead of waiting for the right time, try to realize that usually there *is* no right time—or more simply, *now* is usually the right time. If someone is drowning, you throw them the life jacket *now*. You don't leave to go looking for one with the "right" color.

Domino: Delivering value quickly eliminates fake connections and inauthentic exchanges — and you can use that knowledge to avoid "getting lunch" when nobody really needs or wants to. Use the five-second rule to make sure you take quick action.

Question for you: How much of your time could you put toward more important things if you consistently applied the five-second rule in your life?

AVOID THE "WISHFUL THINKING" TRAP

As I mentioned, nobody on earth is walking around interpreting patterns and reading situations accurately 100 percent of the time. We're not robots, and we all have a host of cognitive distortions that we have to navigate around.

But even if you manage to reframe your own point of view and listen to other people's opinions so you can deliver value faster and better, there are still other mental traps to fall into. One of the worst I can think of is the "wishful thinking" trap.

In wishful thinking, you act as if what I said about not reading situations accurately is not true. Instead, you take as fact that your point of view and your interpretation of the world are solid and unquestionable—whether positive or negative.

For example, here's how this might look from a negative way of thinking. Let's imagine you have a negative self-belief that you just can't shake. Because of early life experiences, you think you're unlovable or uncool or that people don't want to hear what you have to say. Because you accept your own belief as true, it affects your behavior in social situations.

You interact with other people and you understand their wants to the degree you can, but whenever you think of adding value or making connections, you stop yourself. *I'm unlovable and nobody wants to hear what I want to say,* your brain says.

As a corollary to that, you might start to imagine scenarios that *might* happen to you in the future to avoid the pain of dealing with your faulty self-beliefs. *Maybe one day someone will see my real value,* you think. *When the right person comes along, maybe I'll be discovered and appreciated for who I really am.*

The result of this pattern is that you get stuck in your head and life leaves you on the sidelines. You have created a perfect trap for yourself, one that you can't even see.

But the even trickier thing is that the trap doesn't have to be a negative belief. It can also be a positive one!

Let's imagine instead that you are an artist or actor or musician, and you have a powerful inner belief that you are the best at your craft. Often, that positive belief will bleed over into other things and distort the way you view reality.

At a social event, you might talk only about yourself because you view yourself as the most interesting person in the room. *Why wouldn't these people want to hear about me?* you might ask yourself. *I'm going to be the most famous actor in the world one day, and they'll have a great story to tell about when they met me!*

In this situation, maybe your chosen personality turns people off and you never catch your big break—but your self-confidence keeps you going. *I'm going to get discovered,* you think. *There's no way I couldn't be—I'm too talented to be ignored!*

In both cases, the wishful thinking basically amounts to saying: "I don't have to change. I deserve what I want, so something good is going to happen to me eventually." It's funny that a lot of people would quickly call the second example narcissism and the first one depression, but isn't that thought narcissistic no matter what the context is?

The point of all this is to keep the focus on giving *value* on the spot. If you're always sharing what you think with other people and still don't seem to be making good connections or moving ahead, you may be "on the spot," but what you're giving may not be *valuable* to the people around you.

On the other hand, if you're constantly quiet about your ideas and hesitant to make connections with others, you may have a lot of value to add, but you're not being very "on the spot" about it. Falling into either version of this trap should be avoided!

> **Domino:** Avoid wishful thinking that you'll get "discovered" or that everything will magically change for you one day. Instead, market yourself and your value to others.

> **Questions for you:** In what parts of your life are you hesitant to market or "sell" yourself and why? Do any of the reasons have to do with secret wishful thinking?

EVEN GOOD PRODUCTS NEED GOOD MARKETING

Many people have probably heard the old saying "If a product is good enough, it doesn't need any marketing!"

It might sound catchy, but it's just not true—not in business and not in life.

The quintessential example of a product being so "good" (in other words, the customers like it so much) that it doesn't need to be marketed is illicit drugs. But even in that case, it isn't true.

If you look at the history of drug use in the world, there are bubbles for drugs of all kinds. Once upon a time, opium was popular. Later, it was cocaine. Eighty years ago, marijuana was looked at with extremely harsh eyes; now it's being legalized in many places and is nearly mainstream.

If all those different drugs are "good" products, then why aren't they all equally popular all the time? The answer is that the culture, the law, society's understanding of them, the people using them, the traumas people and society are going through at any given time, and so many other things changed over time. In other words, *their marketing changed.*

We cite this rule in other arenas too, like writing or painting—but often, we're just rewriting history when we do that, imagining that certain writers or painters would have risen to the top of the heap on talent alone (although many of them didn't become famous or sell any paintings until after they died).

Jackson Pollock was talented, yes, but he also painted *a lot* and was close friends with art critic Clement Greenberg, who helped push him into the spotlight. Ernest Hemingway was a great writer, yes, but he also developed a very distinctive style in his writing and personal life and befriended dozens of other famous writers—including Gertrude Stein, F. Scott Fitzgerald, James Joyce, and so on.

In *every* case, there is a ton of hard work, marketing, and branding that goes into world-class success.

You could argue that raw talent doesn't need much marketing in professional athletes, where all that counts is your practice and abilities—but then again, at the highest level of competition, marketing and branding play a huge role in getting more opportunities to compete, to train with better trainers, and so on.

In other words, marketing is inescapable.

The point of this is not to discourage anyone who has not yet learned marketing or who doesn't feel like a natural marketer. The point is to blast out any negative thinking that says good things will naturally come to you without any effort or without your influencing anyone else. Because they won't.

On the other hand, embracing the reality that you *do* need to connect with others, you *do* need to show the best side of yourself, and you *do* need to think about what other people think of you (to a degree) can set you free.

It gives you the keys to get out of your own way and start questioning your own view of the world. It softens you up and it makes you more curious, which automatically makes you more fun and interesting to be around.

Once that happens, you find yourself in more situations where you can propel yourself and other people forward. And once you're in those situations, you can act fast.

You can give value on the spot by closing the gap between perception and reception as quickly as possible. Remember that people's first impression of you isn't something you have no control over. You *do* have control over it by being connected, kind, helpful, and thoughtful.

And even more importantly, you *also* have the power to influence the world around you for the better—but you have to believe it's true first.

> **Domino:** The idea that "good products don't need good marketing" might sound catchy, but it isn't true. Even good products need good marketing — so embrace the reality that you do need to make an effort to connect with the outside world in your life and work.

> **Question for you:** What is one life-changing person, product, or service that you would not have heard about without good marketing?

WHEN GIVING VALUE ON THE SPOT GOES WRONG

There are a few different reasons to give value on the spot:

- It demonstrates to other people that you have things to offer and helps to earn their trust right away.

- It works as a "filter" in business and networking situations that gets rid of fake, flaky behavior and incentivizes real connections and action.

- It boosts your relationships and network—and your ability to fold in new relationships and new links in your network.

All of this sounds great and is great in principle, but the downside is there's no guarantee that the people you give value to will have the same positive intentions you do. In short, the effort you put in might not be reciprocated.

It has happened to me again and again over the years.

One of those times was after a Genius Network event I ran, which had high-profile speakers including Arianna Huffington, Tim Ferriss, Darren Hardy, and Dan Sullivan, to name a few. After the event ended, I was doing a brainstorm with Arianna and one of the people I was working with at the time wanted to get involved in our discussion as well. This person and I were friends, and I thought the connection would be useful, both to him and to Arianna, so I brought him into the project.

After that, we ended up working together to help market Arianna's book *Thrive*, which then became a *New York Times* bestseller, and he and Arianna became friends as a result of my introduction, and she introduced him to Oprah, securing a deal to do an interview series for her company.

Later, my friend asked Arianna to speak at one of his events that I was also attending. When the day came, I got a call from Arianna asking me to meet her outside the hotel and lead her backstage since she had never been to the venue before. I said it was no problem and went to meet her outside.

I met her and started walking her backstage, but once I got there, someone stopped me. "You're not allowed back here," this person said. I was confused. To resolve the situation, I called my friend and he told his people to let me backstage, saying that he wasn't sure what had happened and being very inviting. Once I was back there, however, he pulled me aside to talk to me.

"Hey, man," he said, "it throws me off if anyone is backstage while I'm doing an interview—do you care if I just interview Arianna by myself?" I said that was fine and walked away.

Later, Tony Robbins came to do an interview with me at one of my Genius Network Annual Events as a thank-you because I'd helped him with the marketing of his book *Money: Master the Game*. The original plan had been for Tony to spend time with Genius Network members, but this friend asked me if he could interview Tony privately instead.

As a show of good faith, I let him do the interview, and everything went reasonably well, even if it was frustrating for me. After it was over and Tony was talking to my team, one of my other friends who had seen everything unfold came up to talk to me.

"You guys are great," he said, "but that dude is a fucking taker."

After the event, though that person kept partnering with people in Genius Network and making business deals, our relationship became increasingly distant.

Years later, I found out from someone who had worked for him that on the day of the Arianna Huffington event, he had instructed some of his team members to keep me away from Arianna and not to let me backstage. This confused me beyond belief. Why would he do that? What could I have done to cause that kind of insecurity? All I had done was given him value as fast as I could, over and over again.

In essence, giving value on the spot is a surefire way to push yourself and your relationships forward in so many ways—but like anything else, it has its own downsides.

Primarily, the lesson you'll learn the more you put it into practice is that not everybody gives or demonstrates value in the same way. Other times, people only show up to *take* the value you have to give with no intention of paying it back.

Does that mean you should be stingier with people or not make introductions? Of course not—though it is a matter of personal choice and motivation.

My life and success have been about connecting the dots, getting great people in the same room together, and "letting people in." It's no fun to become successful by hoarding your wealth, your connections, or your opportunities without giving other people opportunities as well and seeing what they do with them.

At least, that's how I feel. Just know not everybody feels the same way.

I still recommend assuming good intentions from people and helping out however you can and whenever you want to. The key is to realize that sometimes that effort won't be appreciated. Over time, making effort or giving value without appreciation isn't a relationship. It's being taken advantage of.

Delivering value on the spot is great when you do it for and with the right people. Once you see that's not the case, get out—there are more great people out there who *will* appreciate what you have to offer!

Domino: Giving value on the spot is a guaranteed way to push relationships forward — though not always equally or reciprocally. Still, don't let negativity or takers deter you from finding and connecting with people who will appreciate you.

Questions for you: What beliefs have prevented you from giving value on the spot in the past? Are any of those beliefs still worth holding on to?

The Dominoes:

- When offering someone else help, **deliver value on the spot** by putting your plans in motion immediately.

- **Value depends on urgency.** If you know many high-status or influential people but neither of you does anything to help the other, that value is not real.

- Delivering value requires **learning about other people.** Social media has automated this process, although enabling connection in ways that were previously not possible can also make us detached and lazy. To change that, we have to relearn these skills, apply these skills, and be interested and curious about people again.

- Delivering value quickly eliminates fake connections and inauthentic exchanges—and you can use that knowledge to avoid "getting lunch" when nobody really needs or wants to. Use the **five-second rule** to make sure you take quick action.

- **Avoid wishful thinking that you'll get "discovered"** or that everything will magically change for you one day. **Instead, market yourself and your value to others.**

- The idea that "good products don't need good marketing" might sound catchy, but it isn't true. Even good products need good marketing—so embrace the reality that you do need to make an effort to connect with the outside world in your life and work.

> • **Giving value on the spot is a guaranteed way to push relationships forward—though not always equally or reciprocally.** Regardless, don't let negativity deter you from finding and connecting with people who appreciate you.

Exercises and Action Steps

1. Filling Out Your Own Mackay 66

As mentioned, the Mackay 66 is a list of 66 questions salespeople can use to better understand the people they're selling to. If you're not familiar with it already, do a search online for the full thing or buy Harvey Mackay's book *Swim with the Sharks without Being Eaten Alive*. Some of the questions in his questionnaire (slightly paraphrased) include:

- Did the customer go to college? If so, where? What clubs and extracurriculars did they join?

- If the customer didn't go to college, are they sensitive about that?

- Would your customer object to anyone buying a meal for them? Why or why not?

- What confidential or sensitive items should you not discuss with the customer?

The survey is useful in marketing, but the principles behind it are also useful for your relationships as a guide to how to give more value on the spot.

Questions like these can give us a lot of information about other people; of course, some of this information is now captured by social media algorithms, where we take it for granted.

We tend to look at social media feeds and *think* we know people—without doing the work of gathering and interpreting that information for ourselves. In reality, what we're usually doing is creating some kind of mental stereotype, or buying into someone else's *projection* of who they really are.

To fix those blind spots, getting out a pen and paper to fill out the Mackay 66 for new connections or potential customers is a mind-expanding exercise in just how much we have to learn about the people around us—and how that information can help us be more useful and valuable to them.

2. High-Risk Indicators of HALF (Hard, Annoying, Lame, and Frustrating)

This started when I had lunch with Chris Voss and André Norman to talk about new projects and the topic of finding people who are ELF (easy, lucrative, and fun) instead of HALF came up.

It occurred to me how strange it was to have the three of us together—Chris was the former top international FBI hostage negotiator, now the most sought-after negotiation expert in the world, and André was an ex-convict turned advocate, author, and speaker!

On one level, I took it as evidence of my own abilities to connect people from any walk of life through Genius Network. But it was also proof that if you can get groups of ELF people together, they can find common ground, overcome any differences, and collaborate.

To do that, of course, you have to avoid HALF people in relationships and business negotiations, which can be harder than it sounds. Fortunately, with his negotiating expertise, Chris was able to take my ELF concept and create what he calls "high-risk indicators of HALF" when interacting with others.

According to Chris, one of the biggest telltale signs of HALF sounded like something ELF:

"This could be a great opportunity for you."

In the absence of an actual plan, of other people's successes as examples to follow, or of other concrete details, this usually means that *you* are the opportunity for *them*—and that you will end up doing a ton of HALF work so they can reap the ELF results.

When you constantly give value on the spot (or are surrounded by people who seem to be doing the same thing), it's important to remain at least a little skeptical or critical. Someone who offers to introduce you to someone you've been trying to meet without any strings attached is a good example of *value on the spot*—but someone selling you wild dreams of success without a concrete plan is more likely an example of giving you *trouble on the spot*.

To avoid too much of the latter, you need to sort out the ELF from the HALF—and you can do so by making a list of your own high-risk indicators of HALF. Here's how:

1. **Think back to people you dealt with whom you read entirely wrong and who made your life more HALF. What did they say and do in their early interactions with you that**

sold you on them? Although we all have these interactions with people, we often forget how things started off or fail to look at them with a critical eye. Write down as many examples in as much detail as you can here.

2. **In each of those cases, what were the first red flags (or even yellow flags) that your relationship was on the decline or would fail to improve? What rationalization did you use to ignore them at the time?** Often when we extend our own goodwill and trust to other people when we think they might not deserve it, we know it at the time—we just ignore our better instincts and make the mistake anyway. With each of the examples from step 1, try to remember and record all the moments like this in each one.

3. **Compare your examples and details. What similarities do you see between them? Do any phrases or actions come up again and again? What conclusions can you draw?** No two people are alike, and what's ELF and HALF for each person will vary as well. Still, by looking at the unpleasant relationships and experiences we've had in detail, we can spot patterns—both in other people's bad behavior and in our own weaknesses.

With the answers you have from 3, don't make the same mistakes or ignore your own patterns of behavior or the patterns of behavior you see in others. First, make some notes of how you are *most likely* to be taken advantage of.

After that, write down what *other people* are most likely to say or do to you to exploit that weakness.

From that information, whenever someone says or does one of the things you noted in the early stages of your relationship, you know what to think, *This is a high-risk indicator of HALF for me.*

As Chris Voss says, success is not only about who you spend time with—it's also about who you *consciously* don't waste time on. For more on these concepts and my interviews with Chris, visit www.JoePolish.com/WIIFT.

Chapter 9

GET AS CLOSE TO IN-PERSON AS YOU CAN

Some years ago, I was doing a training in Pittsburgh with some professional cleaners. The group was my platinum level, the highest-level group for the clients I worked with in that industry, and the discussion was about marketing.

The talk was an event connected with the *I Love Marketing* podcast, and most of the audience were familiar with the show. Toward the end of the talk, I told the room that to really practice honing their marketing skills, they should take action on their own.

"We have a lot of curriculum on *I Love Marketing* teaching direct response marketing and plenty of other subjects," I said, "but you have to keep practicing and learning with other people. To do that, you have to start your own meetup groups!"

The idea behind *I Love Marketing* groups worked on a lot of different levels. On one level, it was great organic community building and organizing for the show itself, which in turn was a benefit for podcast co-host Dean Jackson and me.

On another level, it worked exactly the way I was saying: it helped people internalize concepts on their own time, at their own speed—like this idea of starting meetups.

By doing meetups, entrepreneurs and fans of the show could re-create the experience of being in person with me or Dean Jackson by being in person with each other. Beyond that, the mere fact of being in a meetup was an automatic way to get positioned as a leader.

Automatically, that in-person event created great connections and community. It generated opportunities for joint ventures, money-making opportunities, and the potential for lifelong friends.

Finally, the reason it was so great was that it was a way to scale one of the most important principles in life and business: in your interactions, you should get as close to in-person as you can.

WHAT IN-PERSON MEANS AND WHY IT MATTERS

If you remember me describing my texting habits earlier, you may already have a good idea of what I mean by getting as "close to in-person" as possible.

In essence, it means closing the distance between you and another person by any means available—and making every experience you have with someone else as impactful as it can be.

While getting in-person with someone for real isn't always possible, that doesn't mean we have to sacrifice genuine connections with others when we can't really be there with them.

It means that rather than sending stock e-mails or messages, you send heartfelt ones—or you write actual postcards and letters. Instead of boring texts, you send video and audio messages highlighting what you're doing, or showing things that they would find useful. Maybe you even talk on the phone or have an in-person or Zoom meeting to get into dialogue instead of just monologue.

It means adjusting your tone, your body language, and anything else to improve your ability to connect with them in any medium. After all, you need a different kind of communication for each kind of person you meet.

There's a meme online going around that has a well-known piece of wisdom printed on it. I've seen a few different versions, but this is the basic idea:

> *Ninety percent of communication problems in life are due to tone of voice. It's not what you say; it's how you say it that creates the problem.*

It's true in any situation, but it's particularly true when you're not in person. After all, how many times have you had someone misread or misinterpret an e-mail or text?

The bottom line is that tone can make or break a connection—and as we've already established, connection is usually the most important thing that we should all be trying for.

Being enthusiastic is great, but if you come off as *too* enthusiastic, people think you're fake or needy or whatever else. It's like a radio transmitter. When it's tuned perfectly, you can hear the music clearly; when it's not, all you get is static.

Because everyone has their own personality, everyone has their own version of getting close to in-person. If you were to ask me how I communicate with others and how I get "in-person" with people, a lot of these lessons are flashing through my head. The observations about stimulating people's emotions and awakening or agitating desires are particularly important!

As an example of this, before the iPhone existed, the Flip Video came out. The product was a small, boxy hand-held camera that let you take short videos, upload them, and share them quickly.

Right away, I would film tons of Flip videos and e-mail them to people. From the earliest time I could, I was sending audio and video messages to people because I could see how much more effective it was. It stirred much stronger emotions than just text did—and that led to stronger actions from them.

In fact, I remember someone signing up to my $10,000-a-person Genius Network Annual Event along with their partner just based on a voice text I sent them—and I had not seen them in over a decade! But because I sent them an audio telling them to come to the event by going to my website and signing up, they became a Genius Network member.

Just like plants and gardens, friendships and relationships require water. They need sunshine. It's why I always try to remember to keep a constant "drip" of attention and appreciation on the people I care about by writing them notes, sending audio and video messages, and so much else. It makes all the difference.

Domino: Being "in-person" means closing the emotional distance in your relationships in any way possible.

Relationships are like plants: they need a constant "drip" of attention, appreciation, and engagement to grow.

Questions for you: Have any of your close relationships grown less "in-person" over time? What strategies could you use to close that emotional distance?

THE FOUNDATION OF A STRONG IN-PERSON CONNECTION

When I was going to interview John Mackey, the founder of Whole Foods, at one of my Genius Network Annual Events, I wanted to be prepared. More importantly than that, I wanted John to know I cared about his experience at Genius Network.

I knew a lot about John because I'd had a three-hour private lunch meeting with him in 2013 at the Whole Foods headquarters in Austin, Texas (and later, I attended one of his Conscious Capitalism events). Even so, I wanted to figure out and learn as much more about him as I could—so my team and I did a lot of research on his likes and dislikes.

When John showed up to speak, we had a basket in his room with his favorite foods, drinks, DVDs, books, and I can't even remember what else. To get to that point, someone I work with, JR, had watched as many interviews with John as he could and put together some of the very best questions I could ask.

I remember talking to John's assistant, and she forwarded me his comments about the event:

> *I thoroughly enjoyed being at this conference. Joe and his team did a great job. The questions Joe asked*

in his interview were the best questions I have ever been asked in a public forum.

(To see my interview with John Mackey, visit www .JoePolish.com/WIIFT.)

The point of the story is that if you do the work to position things properly, you can make a great impression on someone that leads to incredible results. It isn't about being a smooth talker, either; it's about *caring*.

So many high-level people have other entrepreneurs and fans who want to meet them, but often that second group doesn't even do any research. With John, after he saw the basket we put together for him, he realized that we had invested hours of our lives into making him as comfortable as possible.

It reminds me of Robert Collier's copywriting principle, which I'll repeat: "Enter the conversation that already exists in a prospect's mind." Just like personalized marketing, getting close to in-person comes from personalized connecting and networking.

At this stage in my life, I get so many requests to be interviewed or be on podcasts. When someone reaches out to my team or runs into me in person and asks, "Can I interview you for my podcast?" I ask, "Have you listened to any of my other podcasts?" On the strength of that question, most of the time, I end up turning down most podcast invitations. The truth is, I only invest in people who invest in me. There are simply too many requests and this is just one of the ways that we filter them. It's not the only criterion, but it's a big one.

However, if someone shows up with a genuine, researched, appreciated perspective about what I have to say, then it can be different. I like to say, "Many people want you to eat their dog food when they haven't eaten your dog food." But that's not the way strong connections work.

My friend Robert Cialdini wrote the book *Pre-Suasion* as well as the best-selling *Influence: The Psychology of Persuasion*. Both books have a lot to say on this topic, the latter especially.

Two of Robert's core principles of influence are *liking* and *reciprocity*. They are the same things I advocate here. I'm a big believer in connecting with people by discovering what they are interested in and taking a sincere interest in doing cool things for them. Of course, for it to be a true connection, that energy must be reciprocated as well.

> **Domino:** To make a great impression on others and make them feel special, do your homework. Don't ask anyone to do anything for you without creating value for them first. Don't show up with an entitled attitude. Show them that you care by learning as much as you can about them. By making people feel special, you set a foundation for great relationships — though they must be reciprocal.
>
> **Questions for you:** When you first interact with a new person, what do you expect from them? Do you also expect the same from yourself?

THE WRONG (AND RIGHT) WAYS TO CONNECT IN PERSON AND NEARLY IN-PERSON

If I'm out with somebody who knows another one of my friends, we'll record an audio, shoot a short video, or snap a picture together. In those moments (especially on video), I'll record something funny—of myself, the person I'm with, or both of us—just to say hello, and then I'll send the video to the mutual friend.

I'm constantly facilitating other people's reconnections and conversations, many of whom already know each other. Why? Because it's awkward for a lot of people to reach out even though they would love to connect with the other person. It's part of my philosophy of staying connected by bringing value, utility, and *fun* into situations. Of course, that's just my way. Some people may think I'm weird or too spontaneous. However, I'm a catalyst for making lots of things happen with people that would not happen if I did not operate this way.

When it comes to connecting, it should be all about attitude and energy—which can include enthusiasm, cooperativeness, and friendliness, as well as bantering, sarcasm, and punking your friends, among other things. To connect in-person with good energy, you should seek to understand others first rather than seeking to be understood. Part of that is not being overly argumentative or lording your beliefs over people (unless you know your audience and have rapport—then you can be as weird and extreme as the situation allows).

I often see mistakes made there by people in the nonprofit world. Often, people from nonprofits approach you by explaining that you should fund, donate, or care about their cause for no reason other than it's what they do. They're looking for contribution without enrollment, but they skip the part about making the donor *care*.

People have to be enrolled in the process, and you can't force a butterfly out of a cocoon before it's ready. It's the same thing with building rapport. There's a gestation period and a certain amount of time that needs to be invested.

You have to be patient. You need to look at the entire life cycle of a relationship or project and you can't try to take shortcuts. This is usually fine for people who are givers anyway—but anyone who feels entitled is going to struggle here.

Of course, all of this comes to the counterpoint: what *not* to do.

In short, the wrong ways to connect in-person include being too pushy or being persistent to the point of annoyance or driving someone away. That includes being cocky (unless you have rapport with them), arrogant, and self-serving, especially to the detriment of the other person.

Another danger is when somebody *pretends* they know someone else but ends up straining their supposed relationship or rapport. It can happen either when someone's misreading a situation or when someone's coming from a place of insecurity—and the latter is a more serious issue, because to really connect with people, you have to build up a sense of security in yourself. You have to know that you bring value to situations and you have to want to share it with other people.

Of course, you must also have discretion.

There are a lot of people who want me to connect them to people I know without providing something of value that makes the connection make sense, or before they're really at those people's level. What I tell them is to write something up that I can show the person they want to connect with, because I can't make introductions based on half-baked requests. There has to be a good reason and a benefit for everyone involved. Plus, if the connection is important to them and the person requesting it, it's not my job to do all the work for them.

Naturally, for every rule and "right way," there are just as many examples of people getting success doing the opposite. In other words, there are people who get what they want in life because they're really persistent and annoying. Still, while they sometimes get what they want, they also turn people off.

People don't think very highly of annoying people, even if annoying people *are* often high in the ranks of power. While persistence *can* get you what you want, if it's your *only* strategy, it goes against the whole message of this book.

Everyone has different strengths, but if there is one "right" way to do things, it's to know in advance the outcome for the other person—and know what will make them lean in to you. The right way to get as close to in-person as you can is to be well positioned, high-status (earned, not faked), valuable, and useful so people want to go deeper and learn more about you.

> **Domino:** Making other people feel special and appreciated is a way to connect—but it's equally important to know what not to do. Though there's no one "right" way to do things, choose behaviors that make people want to lean toward you, not away from you.

> **Questions for you:** In your closest relationships, what are the behaviors you do that make other people "lean" toward you? How different can these behaviors look across your relationships?

TREAT MORE CONVERSATIONS LIKE THEY ARE CRUCIAL

Let's face it: A lot of the conversations we have in life are just for the sake of conversation. In other words, while we might make some connections and have fun, we wouldn't call them *crucial* conversations.

We don't have that many crucial conversations in life, but when we do, think about what those tend to look like. Maybe it's negotiating a raise with a boss, or maybe it's breaking up with someone in a relationship that has gone sour. Whatever the situation, most of these conversations have to do with the values that are most important to us—the things we would die for.

These pivotal conversations are so important to get right that there's a whole book called *Crucial Conversations* by Joseph Grenny and Kerry Patterson dedicated to the strategy behind them.

Though there is a lot more detail in the book than we can go into here, one of the topics it covers is establishing a connection and agreeing on things when possible. This is what's called (in a phrase you've surely heard) *common ground*.

It's a question worth considering in crucial conversations, but it's actually important in all conversations: *Where's the common ground?* Even if you *completely* disagree with someone politically or on some other basis, where can mutual respect come in? Answering that question can unlock ways to be useful and valuable.

For me, as I think about these points, the question becomes: *Why don't we treat all of our conversations as crucial?* Unless you're just making small talk, there's no reason not to. And something is lost when we don't. Because we often don't treat conversations as crucial, many people have trouble connecting with others.

The idea I'm getting across here is that even if a conversation *isn't* crucial, do we lose anything by being more open to it or more present in it? We tend to look for what seem like the ideal situations and scenarios to deploy our best selves. But what if we just led with our best, no matter what?

If you see a wilting plant that needs two cups of water and you only have one cup of water, that cup of water will still help the plant. Connecting is like that: pouring water on plants. Even if you don't think you have quite enough water to give in the moment. And no matter how successful people are, they often don't put enough effort into nourishing, nurturing, giving sunshine, watering, and harvesting their relationships.

> **Domino:** Deeper connections are formed by finding common ground. To do so, identify what is core to you—and then treat more conversations you have like they are crucial, in accordance with your values.

> **Questions for you:** What kinds of conversations in your life do you tend to rush through? If you slowed down for some of them and found new ways to connect, what kind of an impact could that make?

BE REAL, NOT COSMETIC

As I mentioned earlier, my connections with many high-level people have come from putting in the reps doing what I've been writing about in this book for many years, knowing how to speak their language, offering value on the spot, and drawing on the many other applications from this book to open doors for both parties.

Still, there can sometimes be a downside to offering value and maneuvering through rooms if you're not doing it with a genuine spirit—or if the people around you don't appreciate you.

I once connected with a wealthy entrepreneur on a joint venture to benefit his foundation with some smart marketing. The plan included flying other businesspeople and entrepreneurs out to a beautiful vacation spot that the entrepreneur owned.

The idea was that I could organize entrepreneurial "brainstorm" events at the location for the visitors while the wealthy entrepreneur was also vacationing there. By doing so, the visitors would get some access to and conversation with this entrepreneur in exchange for paying a high fee.

The first year, we charged $45,000 per person, or $75,000 per couple, to attend our all-inclusive events. Right away, the plan was a huge success. At the end of the year, we gave all the profits to the entrepreneur—a total of close to half a million dollars going to his foundation.

Over the years, my team and I kept bringing people to the location. To create value above and beyond renting out his property and sharing profits, I also raised millions for his organizations and foundation through various marketing and outreach efforts, all of which reached thousands of people.

I was doing what I had always done: being inclusive and getting people in the mix. The problem was, sometimes that energy wasn't as reciprocal as I hoped it would be.

From my perspective, the entrepreneurs I was bringing in were generating a ton of value and opportunities for the wealthy entrepreneur. In the meantime, I was also boosting the careers of people I introduced to him. Even so, all the effort and value wasn't translating into the entrepreneur or his team associating with or joining Genius Network.

Eventually, I just asked them outright:

"Everything you're doing with the people I'm bringing over seems to go so well. Why don't you guys come to Genius Network? You could do so much more with us!"

Usually they said they were interested, but it never materialized. Later, I also found out that even though it was my assistant, Eunice, who was booking and coordinating everything for the trips, the entrepreneur's camp was paying a travel agency a 15 percent kickback—but they weren't doing any of the work!

Though I kept up a friendly relationship with the entrepreneur, I eventually stopped doing the trips because of my mixed feelings and passed the model and the business in its entirety over to a friend of mine who was still passionate about it.

I remembered that a few years prior, the entrepreneur had thrown a high-profile fundraiser for his foundation. Tickets were expensive and there were some 600 people attending, about 200 of whom my team and I had brought there. In the audience were many high-level entrepreneurs whom I'd done great business with over the years.

My team members and I helped put the event together and we were going to be seated at a table with the entrepreneur, but we were surprised when his team told us we couldn't attend as his guests. Instead, we were asked to pay $2,500 each for our seats.

The core part of the event was a big charity auction of expensive collector's items, and I encouraged my guests to bid. In all, the people my team and I brought in accounted for more than 60 percent of the auction sales.

At the end of the night, the entrepreneur got onstage with a smile and thanked everyone. While he was up there, he called out every celebrity in the room by name, letting the crowd give them a warm round of applause and appreciation.

Since it was a big event, there were celebrities invited to emcee and make a splash. Though we thought nothing of it at the time, my team and I found out after the event that none of the celebrities attending had to pay to be there.

The feeling of alienation I felt in the room that night and days after stuck with me. I was looking at a room full of faces that had all paid to be there, to give money to what I hoped to be a good cause and to be as in-person as possible. But not everyone in the room had the same motivations.

It was a hard lesson to learn that people can be literally and physically in person with you and still *not* be "in-person."

In all parts of life, we have ideals and expectations about how we should be or how things should go. Generally, if we could have it all our way, things would always turn out rosy and optimistic—even if it doesn't go that way in reality.

In trying to make our wildest dreams a reality, sometimes we consciously or unconsciously present a fake version of ourselves to try to win favor or sway someone. Other times, we maintain relationships with people that we wouldn't otherwise, hoping we might get something from it.

In those situations, we might still be following the principles of giving value on the spot or getting close to in-person, but we're doing it in a cosmetic way. It's not coming from a genuine place.

Giving value and connecting with others is half the game, but the other half is that energy gets cycled between two parties for their benefit. It means you give something and the energy is *reciprocated*.

Reciprocity comes from being useful or providing somebody solutions, gifts, and humor, but it also relies on you being *genuine*. The right way to go about all this is to not be cheap with your time, money, attention, and energy. What's effective is being a *giver* to the right people, as opposed to a taker.

As all successful people eventually learn, the motivation and drive that got you successful doesn't always sustain you once you're at the top. Even up there, there are still plenty of people secretly playing out their own status games.

No matter who it is or where you go, you will find people nursing their own private wounds and insecurities and taking it out on others.

In successful circles with high-level people, that can often mean that people treat you well enough to get what they want while always keeping you on the outside. It also means that successful people have to build a thick shell around themselves to prevent that.

I was talking to a friend of mine who married a famous director. As she explained to me, people often invite her to events and act like they want to include her, but more often than not, she can tell it's only because they want to get to her husband.

All those people are focused on themselves, and all they care about is what a connection with my friend will do for them—never considering her emotions or how she feels about it.

By now, so many people have tried to use her to get to her husband that she has become very perceptive. Those skills of observation are a great consolation prize, but in my humble opinion, being treated like a human being is better.

Domino: You can be in person with people without being "in-person." Monitor your relationships and environment to be sure that people's actions toward you are genuine rather than surface level. Avoid cosmetic behavior in your own relationships as well, as they cause compounding resentment.

Questions for you: When was the last time you were far away from someone but they made you feel like you were in person? Similarly, when was the last time you really were in person but they made you feel far away? (Note: I can already hear the criticism that no one can "make" you feel anything, but some powerful people can certainly control the environment around you so much that it starts to feel that way.)

SELF-AWARENESS AND CONSISTENCY

Understanding the need to go beyond shallow or boilerplate communication will take you a long way, but executing that idea can take you even farther.

One way to think of it is that writing one postcard to someone or sending one birthday text may produce a positive result, but it isn't enough to get maximum results from this principle. You have to embrace the entire idea and make it your way of being in the world rather than something you only do here and there.

What you do at any given moment is valuable in itself, but the sum of all those moments helps you build a reputation as a caring and useful person. While value in the moment is great on its own, becoming known as someone who gives value everywhere and all the time is even better.

To keep it simple, how often you close the distance between people—and the way you do it—matters.

How you spend your time matters. Who you spend your time with matters, even when you're goofing around. After all, we all get enthusiastic about different things in life, and often those things are the very energy source we need to tap into to bridge the gap with others. We also need those sources of energy for ourselves when things don't go our way.

In trying to be as "in-person" as possible, you will likely make mistakes, get rejected, and say the wrong thing. Your ability to course correct when that happens—to say sorry, brush yourself off, and move on— is critically important. Being willing to realize you could be going down the wrong path is an important awareness to develop.

In all cases, be your own best friend. The more you can be your own best friend, the better friend, parent, partner, husband, wife, sibling, and whatever else you will be! Give yourself and other people some slack. Know your life will improve to the degree you care about it and treat yourself with respect.

What makes your life better is not someone else's value system or someone else trying to convince you their way is the right way. Just look at what's working for you and do more of what's working. And remember that it's not just about doing things right. It's about doing the right things with the right people.

Domino: Going beyond basic communication with people will take you a long way, but executing that concept in all areas of life with self-awareness and creativity is what will take you the farthest.

Questions for you: How much creativity do you put into your daily communication with other people? What are some ways that you could make your interactions with other people more exciting?

The Dominoes:

- Being **"in-person" means closing the emotional distance** in your relationships in any way possible. **Relationships are like plants:** they need a constant "drip" of attention, appreciation, and engagement to grow.

- To make a great impression on others and make them feel special, **do your homework**. Show them that you care by learning as much as you can about them. **By making people feel special, you set a foundation** for great relationships—though they must be reciprocal.

- Making other people feel special and appreciated is a way to connect—but it's equally important to know what *not* to do. Though there's no one "right" way to do things, **choose behaviors that make people want to lean toward you, not away from you.**

- **Deeper connections are formed by finding common ground.** To do so, identify what is core to you— and then **treat every conversation you have like it is crucial**, in accordance with your values.

- **You can be in person with people without being "in-person."** Monitor your relationships and environment to be sure that people's actions toward you are genuine rather than surface level. **Avoid cosmetic behavior in your own relationships** as well, as they cause compounding resentment and produce low self-esteem.

• **Going beyond boilerplate communication** with people will take you a long way, but executing that concept in all areas of life **with self-awareness and creativity is what will take you the farthest**.

Exercises and Action Steps

1. The Genius Network Introduction

In Genius Network groups, we sometimes invite everyone to fill out a simple introduction card before fully interacting and networking with each other at each event. In fact, it's an exercise we have to credit world-class speaker, speaking coach, and Genius Network member Joel Weldon, who introduced it to Genius Network. Though this may seem simple, the reason we do them is so our members can be as *in-person* as possible with one another in a way that gives value on the spot.

To do the introduction card yourself, answer the following:

1. **After writing down your name, write <u>what you have</u>.** In your interactions with others, what things do you already have that are valuable to other people? They can be physical things or emotional things, but they need

to be at the core of what you do and what you're about.

2. **Write down <u>what you can give</u>.** Extended from the above, what can you offer to other people with those things you have? What experiences do you create for people?

3. **Write down <u>what those things get</u>.** Building off those last two things, what does the combination of steps 1 and 2 lead to? If you described things in your business, what *results* does your business deliver for others? If you wrote down emotional qualities or values, what positive *effect* does your outlook have on the people you interact with?

4. **Write down <u>where you need help</u>.** No matter how good we are, everyone needs help with something. Just as nobody can offer exactly what you offer for steps 1, 2, and 3, your answer here can be complemented by what someone else can bring to the table.

For an example, here's how I filled out mine:

I'm Joe Polish.

I've got two high-level groups, 100K and Genius Network . . .
  . . . that give people opportunities to build an ELF business through impactful discussions and powerful connections . . .
  . . . that get them more profits, better clients, and amazing connections and lead to an extraordinary life.
  I want help expanding my Genius Recovery platform.

With all this information in one place and in the front of your mind, it's nearly impossible to not be entirely in-person with the people you meet.

2. Revisit Your Core Values

We talked about core values back in Chapter 3. Your core values are extremely powerful in helping you find the common ground that leads to deep connection—so this is a perfect time to take a fresh look at what matters most to you. Try this simple exercise:

1. **On a piece of paper, brainstorm the few things (or people) in life that you would truly sacrifice or die for.** Why are they so important to you? Do any of your answers surprise you?

2. **Based on your answers, identify which of those things is the most important of all.** Is there another principle or "rule" that unites everything on the list?

3. **Once you've identified the most important thing or things, work backward: What does that thing tell you about what you believe in?** What does a person who would die for the thing you wrote down believe in? What do they care about? What don't they care about?

Doing this will help you identify values that are core to you as a human being, and that knowledge can help you establish common ground with people you meet and continue asking our central question: *What's in it for them?*

CONCLUSION

Once I was in recovery, my goals were to stay in good physical and mental shape, build a successful business by transforming an entire industry with ethical marketing (which I did), reduce suffering for entrepreneurs, and walk my walk and talk my talk as best as humanly possible. That approach has served me well, and it has made me very aware that some skills in business are way more valuable than others.

There is no relationship between being good and getting paid, but there is a huge relationship between being good, being a good *marketer*, and getting paid.

I've been lucky to be born in a great country and to have been exposed to knowledge that made a huge difference in my life. It was my continual pursuit of the best knowledge and the best relationships that led me to where I am today. I don't want to minimize the fact that I have worked really hard to learn, develop, and apply the skills that got me here, and I hope I've done a decent job conveying those skills throughout this book.

Throughout my life I've made money and lost money, met tons of people who inspire me, had too many painful and exciting experiences to count, and forged connections between other people to spread my impact even further. Still, going so hard for so long can burn anyone out—even me.

In 2021, I announced that I was going on a sabbatical, and this book was largely a product of that downtime.

For as long as I can remember, I've been charging forward without stopping, seeking stimulation, and throwing myself into projects and relationships. In the middle of that, I got away from my roots as a marketer and copywriter—and I stopped writing things down in general (my friends who get voice notes from me all the time can attest to that). In this process, what I've noticed is that writing down what you've learned about business and relationships in your life has a way of making you reflect on things.

When I stepped away from work and business approximately a year ago to continue to work on this book, I was feeling a little disillusioned with the self-help and marketing industry and many of the people the world looks up to as leaders, people who are considered "successful." I had achieved more success than I had ever dreamed of at that time, but my own life was getting more complicated. On top of it all, I was also processing the grief of having a few of the most important people in my life die unexpectedly.

I still wanted to give to the truly amazing helpers and givers in the world and charge forward, but in some ways, I felt like I was losing some of my direction. I wanted to make a shift, but I wasn't sure where. In the middle of that came the COVID-19 pandemic, which has resulted in people losing their jobs and their loved ones as well as mass confusion caused by conflicting media reports, unclear government guidelines, political motivations, massive propaganda, and so many other patterns that I had never seen so clearly in my lifetime.

Conclusion

As 2020 and 2021 charged forward and so many families and friends weren't able to see each other, go to their favorite places, or spend time with loved ones (in the United States and most of the world), a lot of self-evaluation and self-reflection started happening in real time. All over the place, and often on social media, people started wondering if they were making the right choices or leading purposeful lives. Others were severely depressed, suicidal, lonely, and addicted.

And in that space, the world where I spend most of my time sort of lost its mind. I think many people would agree that the same thing happened in their worlds as well.

Post-COVID, we're entering a world that is in the middle of an ideological war. Social media companies and their sorting algorithms have people more remote and divided than ever. We're more distrustful of everything than ever before, and in the process, we're forgetting how to find common ground, talk to each other, and build things together.

When I looked back at my life at the beginning of last year, I was very grateful for what I had, but exhaustion was starting to creep in. I started questioning some of the decisions I'd made, some the relationships I'd been pouring energy into, and personal boundaries that I hadn't enforced enough.

I was not okay with how so much unclear and often dishonest guidance was making life difficult for so many people. The ones being hurt the most were the ones who didn't have the financial means to sustain through the difficulties that people with power were creating. It was demoralizing that so many of our leaders were putting their own interests ahead of the interests of people who were suffering.

It was ironic that I had taken my sabbatical during a pandemic, but the experience still led to a personal awakening for me as it did for so many others.

Seeing the distance that was growing between friends, families, communities, and people all over the world, I remembered what I'd been doing all along and who I was. I was a guy who brought people together. I was a guy who *connected* people.

It's easy to get burned or be deceived by your own ambition, and there are naturally stages in life when you're "in pursuit" and others when you pull back and reflect. I thought I had lost my energy for a while there, but now I feel it coming back again.

As I said at the start of this book, *I knew I didn't only want to write about capabilities; I also wanted to write about character.*

Coming back to the world with a new perspective, I hope this book can help you understand your own character in a way that supports your business, your connections, and your own growth. I hope that it can be the first "domino" for anyone who is looking to embrace entrepreneurship, and that it can help existing entrepreneurs who are still growing and forging their own meaning in the world. For me, I'm hoping my next chapter can be about a focus on being a catalyst to the givers in the world and a way to put up a force field between themselves and the takers.

As I continue to work in more thoughtful, strategic, and intentional ways, I want to continue driving Genius Network forward. I also want to spend more time helping people in recovery from addiction, with projects like Artists for Addicts, Genius Recovery, and GeniusX, my VR company. Heck, I even bought a 40-acre ghost town called Cleator,

Arizona, which a couple of friends and I are rebuilding—check that out at www.WhatsYourCleator.com.

I hope to do more creative work like the work I've done with Akira Chan and others on movies for Artists for Addicts, stories that make an impact on people's hearts while also raising money and being a catalyst for important causes.

To some extent, I also want to share more about the conditions that made me who I am, including recovering from multiple addictions and some early life experiences (many of which are chronicled in the movie Genius Network/100K member Devang Patel and Emmy Award–winning producer Nick Nanton made about my life, *Connected: The Joe Polish Story*).

What I've learned in writing this is that even if the appearance of things changes, the essence stays the same.

People want to connect.

People want to feel special and cared about.

People want to feel appreciated.

People want to have their problems solved.

And if you're a person who cares about others and can solve their problems—someone who understands what's in it for *them*—there's no limit to what you can accomplish or the peace and joy you can find in your own existence.

LESSONS FROM JOE'S SABBATICAL

In 2021 I took a one-year sabbatical. It provided a lot of insight and gave me time to really think and ponder the lessons I learned from it. I'll share a few of them below. If you'd like the whole list of 35-plus Sabbatical Lessons, with deeper explanations of them all, and would like to watch a talk I gave on what I learned, please visit:

www.JoesSabbatical.com

- There are no rules for sabbaticals. You do what you want.

- Be willing to destroy anything in your life that is not excellent.

- Chasing happiness chases it away.

- Not being on social media is healthier for your brain than reading inspirational quotes on social media.

- Unlearning is harder than learning.

- You don't know what you've got 'til it's gone, but you also don't know how much bullshit you put up with until you step away from it for a while.

- It's easier to make personal decisions when you're not burdened with business decisions.

RESOURCES

Remember I mentioned at the beginning of the book that we've set up a simple way for you to access the resources, tools, and exercises you have found in these pages?

Just point your smartphone at the QR code below and it will take you directly to the resources page:

www.WIIFTbook.com/resources

INDEX

A

Action items. *See* Exercises and action steps
Active listening, 94, 95, 107
Addiction and recovery
  boredom and beyond, 151–152
  disconnection and connection, 13–15
  drug "marketing," 194
  laughter and, 147
  mission statement, xvii
  mistreatment example, 125
  Polish's addiction and recovery journey, 13–15, 22–23, 100–101, 229
  suffering and, 3–4, 13–14
  through art and music, 89–90
  trauma bonding and, 70–72
Allen, David, 184
Annoying relationships. *See* HALF relationships
Apathy, 176
Appreciating people, 157–180
  background, 157–159
  dominoes on, 162, 165, 171, 174, 176, 178–179
  effect of, 159–162, 176–178, 179
  exercises and action steps, 179–180
  intimidation and, 165–171
  meaning of, 159–162
  in practice, 157–159, 162–165, 178
  self-appreciation, 174–176, 178–179
  unappreciated and underappreciated people, 172–178
Appreciation Letters exercise, 180
Art and artists, 35, 89–90, 233
Artists for Addicts program, 89–90, 232, 233
Atmospheric conditions, 8–12, 26
Attachment theory, 70–71
Attraction
  to danger and pain, 69–72, 82
  energy of, 61–66, 82
  and repulsion for deepening relationships, 66–69
Authenticity
  appreciation and, 163
  formalities and, 138–140
  how to treat people with, 121–124, 131
  of in-person and nearly-in-person communication, 209–210, 212–213, 218–223
  lessons on, 22–25, 27
  for rapport-building, 21, 95
  selling and, 9–10

B

Bach, David, 57

Baruch, Bernard, 81
Beachbody, 170
"Being connected," 87–91. *See also*
Gratitude; Utility; Value
Black Star (documentary), 89–90
Body for Life (Phillips), 170
Body language, 20, 21, 209
Body of Work (film), 168–170
Bonding with people
through attraction and repul-
sion, 66–69
through laughter, 145–148
trauma bonding, 70–71, 79
Boredom, 150–153, 154
Boundaries and boundary-setting
attachment theory on, 70–71
formalities and, 140
on Not To Do list, 55–57
as self-appreciation, 174–176,
178–179
situational awareness of, 118–
120, 133
Branson, Richard, 51, 111–113,
148, 170
Buddhism, 4
Butcher, Jon, 89

C

Caller ID, 62–63. *See also* Deepen-
ing connections
Campbell, Joseph, 102
Carnegie, Dale, xv
Carpet and FabriCare Institute,
160–161
Chan, Akira, 89, 90, 233
Chan, Amy, 86
Chapman, Gary, 116–117
Childhood trauma, 70–71, 79, 82
Cialdini, Robert, 34, 213
Cleator, Arizona, 233
Clinton, Bill, 148
Clown school, 147
Coast Guard example, 126
Collaborative connection, xvi–xvii,
34–36, 52, 137–138, 139
Collier, Robert, 184, 212

Comfort and comfort zones
defined, 19
expansion of, xix. *See also* Exercises and action steps
rapport-building and, 15,
18–21, 27
situational awareness of,
118–120
Common ground, 217–218, 225,
226–227, 231–232
Communicating
appreciation for people, 157–
159, 178, 180
defined, 10–11
as interaction position, 10–11
rapport-building and, 15–21,
24–25
through tone of voice, 209–210
Complaints and complaining,
116–117
Connected: The Joe Polish Story
(film), 233
Connecting and connections,
87–91. *See also* Networking (general); Networking
principles
Consumer's Guide to Carpet Cleaning
(Polish), 24, 91–93
Core values, 80–82, 228
Corporate artists, 35
Cosmetic behavior, 218–223
COVID-19 pandemic, 230–232
Crucial Conversations (Grenny &
Patterson), 217
Cunningham, Keith, 106
Curiosity
about conflicts, 65, 66
about others' interests, 116–117
about suffering, 6–7, 8–10
negativity and, 195
social media's effect on,
187–188
Customer questionnaire (Mackay
66), 186–187, 201–202

D

"Deal with people at the level at which they respond," 122
Deepening connections, 59–86
    attraction and repulsion for, 66–69
    attraction to danger and pain lessons, 69–72, 82
    attraction-type energy for, 41–42, 61–66, 82
    background example, 59–61
    dominoes on, 61, 66, 68–69, 71, 80, 81–82, 120, 133
    exercises and action steps, 83–86
    people-picker skills for, 72–80, 82
    personal costs for, 80–82
    situational awareness for, 118–120, 133
Discernment, 6–7, 19–20. *See also* Pain detective mindset
Disconnection and disconnecting
    addiction and, 13–15
    as escaping, 10–11
    from what doesn't serve you, 52
Disorganization, 46
"Does this grow the relationship?" 38
Dominatrix, 114–115
Dominoes
    about, xviii, 103–104
    on appreciating people, 162, 165, 171, 174, 176, 178–179
    on deepening connections, 61, 66, 68–69, 71, 80, 81–82, 120, 133
    on ELF relationships (easy, lucrative, and fun), 140, 144, 148, 150, 153, 154
    first dominoes, 103–104, 108–109
    on how to treat people, 113, 115, 117, 120, 124, 126, 132–133
    on in-person connections, 210–211, 213, 216, 218, 223, 225–226
    on investing in relationships, 35–36, 37, 40, 42, 44, 50, 52–53
    mindset for life and relationships, 3, 15, 21, 25, 26–27
    mindset on suffering, 4, 6, 7, 12
    on utility, gratitude, and value, 90, 95, 98, 101–102, 105, 106–107
    on value on the spot, 185, 188, 191, 193, 196, 199–201
Driven to Distraction (Hallowell & Ratey), 34
Drug "marketing," 194

E

Einstein, Albert, 151
ELF relationships (easy, lucrative, and fun)
    about, xvi–xvii
    background, xvi–xvii
    deepening connections for, 62–66
    dominoes on, 52, 53
    exercises and action steps, 54–58
    as first dominoes, 108–109
    Genius Network and, 33–34
    High-risk indicators of HALF and, 202–204
    investment in, 50–52, 53, 54–56, 58
    qualities of, 63–64
Emotional atmosphere, 8–12, 26
Emotional suffering, 3
Empathy
    being connected through, 94–95, 107
    emotional atmosphere determination and, 8–12
    pain detective mindset, 6–7, 8–10, 26, 27–28
    suffering point and, 11–12
    as utility in practice, 94

Energy
    of communication and connec-
        tion, 11
    for deepening connections,
        40–42, 61–66, 82
    of in-person and nearly-in-per-
        son communication,
        214–215
    investment dangers, 47–48
    positivity and, 25
Enrollment in the process,
    214–215
"Enter the conversation that
    already exists in a prospect's
    mind," 212
Entitlement, 97, 103
Escaping, 10–11, 17. *See also* Dis-
    connection and disconnecting
Exercises and action steps
    about, xix
    for appreciating people,
        179–180
    for being connected, 108–109
    for deepening connections,
        83–86
    for ELF relationship develop-
        ment, 155–156
    on how to treat people,
        134–136
    for in-person and nearly-in-per-
        son communication,
        226–228
    for investing in relationships,
        54–58
    on mindset development,
        27–31
    for value on the spot, 201–205
Expression, 35–36, 52

F

Faith, Mike, 112
Fake friends, 48
False images, 48–49
Favors, 21, 163, 172
Fearless Inventory exercise, 83–85
Filling Out Your Own Mackay 66
    exercise, 201–202

Financial recklessness, 48–49
First dominoes, 103–104, 108–109
The Five Love Languages (Chap-
    man), 116–117
Five-second rule, 190–191, 200
Fladlien, Jason, 44
Flip Video, 210
Fogg, BJ, 146–147
Food metaphor, for trauma bond-
    ing, 70–71
Formalities, 138–140, 154
Frederickson, Fabienne, xviii
Frustrating relationships. See HALF
    relationships
Fun. See ELF relationships
Fun relationships. See ELF
    relationships

G

Gambling, 48
The Game (Strauss), 16–17, 18
The Gap and the Gain (Sullivan &
    Hardy), 65
Genius Network
    about, 25, 28–29, 33–34, 42, 44
    background overview, xvii, xviii
    being connected through,
        89–91
    headquarters description, 146
    on how to treat people, 119
    mindset for relationships in,
        8–9
    protocol for joining, 127–129
    rapport-building example,
        139–140
    Return on Genius (Reputation),
        43–44, 53–54
    value-on-the-spot experiences,
        181–182, 197–198
Genius Network creation exercise,
    28–31
Genius Network Introduction exer-
    cise, 226–228
GeniusX, 232
GeniusRecovery.org, 90, 232
Genuineness. *See* Authenticity

Getting-things-done (GTD) method, 184
Ghost town, 232–233
Glickman, Ken, 27
Goals in 90 days, 55–56
Goddard, Neville, 4
Good products, marketing of, 193–196, 200–201
Gratitude (for being connected), 87–109
    background example, 87–91
    dominoes on, 90, 98, 105, 106–107
    exercises and action steps, 108–109
    guide to, 102–105, 107
    in practice, 96–98, 101
    thinking time on, 105–106
Great days, 66
Greenberg, Clement, 194
Grenny, Joseph, 217
Growth, in relationships, 38–40, 43, 53, 55
Growth, personal, 80–82
GTD (getting-things-done) method, 184

Heinlein, Robert, 138–139
Hello Kitty wallet, 143–144
Hemingway, Ernest, 194
High-Risk Indicators of HALF exercise, 202–205
Honesty. See Authenticity
How to treat people, 111–136
    authenticity and, 121–124, 131
    background example, 111–113
    dominoes on, 113, 115, 117, 120, 124, 126, 132–133
    exercises and action steps, 134–136
    "haters" and negativity, 116–117, 127–132, 133
    language of other people, 116–117, 132–133
    mistreatment, 124–126, 133
    situational awareness and behavior, 118–124, 133
    you are not your own customer, 114–116
How to Win Friends and Influence People (Carnegie), xv
Huffington, Arianna, 197–198
Humor, 18, 20, 118–119, 141–148
Hunt-Davis, Ben, 38

H

Habits of humor, 146–148. See also Humor
Halbert, Gary, 28, 66–67, 168–169
HALF relationships (hard, annoying, lame, and frustrating)
    about, xvi
    discernment skills to identify, 19–20
    high-risk indicators for, 202–205
    how to treat, 116–117, 127–132, 133
    investment dangers, 48, 55–56
    underappreciation and unappreciation by, 172–174
Hallowell, Ned, 34
Happy Client Experience, 149–150
Hardy, Ben, 65
"Have a great day!" 139
Headley, Jason, 11

I

I Love Marketing groups, 207–208
I Love Marketing podcast, xviii, 77, 145, 207–208
Identify Your Core Values exercise, 228
If I Could Have It the Way I Want It exercise, 135–136
Illicit drug "marketing," 194
Improv classes, 147, 156
Influence: The Psychology of Persuasion (Cialdini), 213
In-person and nearly-in-person communication, 207–228
    background, 207–208
    cosmetic behavior, 218–223, 225–226
    crucial conversations, 216–218, 225

defined, 208–209
dominoes on, 210–211, 213, 216, 218, 223, 225–226
exercises and action steps, 226–228
foundation of, 211–213, 225
in practice, 209–211, 213–216, 225
self-awareness and consistency, 223–225, 226
Intimidation, 165–171
Inventory exercise, 83–85
Investing in relationships, 33–58
background, 33–34
as collaboration, xvi–xvii, 34–36, 52, 137–138, 139
dangers of, 45–50, 55–57
dominoes on, 35–36, 37, 40, 42, 44, 50, 52–53
exercises and action steps, 54–58
flow and fun of, 50–52, 53, 54–56, 58. *See also* ELF relationships
for growth of deep relationships, 40–42, 43, 53, 54–55
one-sentence solution, 38–40, 43, 52
overview, 42–43
Return on Genius (Reputation), 42–44, 52–53
spending vs. investing mindset, 36–38
Investing vs. spending mindset, 36–38
iPhones, 157–159
It's Not about the Nail (video), 11

J

Jackson, Dean, xviii, 142–144, 145, 182, 208
Jobs, Steve, 35
Jokes, 18, 20, 118–119, 141–144, 145–148

K

Kekich, Dave, 88–89, 90, 98–99, 105
Kekich Credos, 99
Kindness, xix, 7, 10, 25
Kurzweil, Ray, 164

L

Lalla, Annie, 67, 68, 74–77, 86, 148
Lame relationships. *See* HALF relationships
Language of other people, 116–117, 132–133
Laughter, power of, 145–148. *See also* Humor
Leeches, 48. *See also* HALF relationships
"Life gives to the giver," 44
Lists. *See* Not Now List; Not To Do List
Long-term investments, 36–38, 52
Love language, 116–117
Lucrative relationships. *See* ELF relationships

M

Mackay 66 (customer questionnaire), 186–187, 201–202
Mackay, Harvey, 79, 185–187, 201–202
Mackey, John, 211–212
Magic Rapport Formula, xviii. *See also* Networking principles
"Make it a great day!" 139
Make Your Own List of Riffs exercise, 155–156
Manners, 138–140, 154
Mastermind model, xvii. *See also* Genius Network
Memorable impressions, 149–150, 154
Mental anguish (suffering), 3

Mindset for life and relationships, 1–31
background, 1–3
connection and disconnection, 10–11, 13–15
dominoes on mindset, 3, 4, 6, 7, 12, 15, 21, 25, 26–27
emotional atmosphere determination, 8–12, 26
exercises and action steps, 27–31
Genius Network creation, 25, 28–31
inauthenticity lessons, 22–25, 27. See also Authenticity
pain detective mindset, 6–7, 8–10, 12, 19–20, 27–28
on suffering, 3–6. See also Suffering
transactional mindset, xv, xvi, 9–10, 36–38, 51
transformative relationships, 36–38
trust, rapport, and comfort for, 15–21, 27
for value on the spot, 181–205. See also Value (on the spot)
Minimum effective dose, 123–124
Mirroring, 64–65, 122–123, 124, 134–135
Mistreatment, 124–126, 133
Money, 36–38, 48–51, 54–55
Muscle Media (magazine), 169–170

N

Negative thinking, 152–153, 191–192, 195
Negativity and "haters," 65, 116–117, 127–132, 133
Networking (general)
connecting defined, 10–11
disclaimers, xix
dominoes and, xviii. See also Dominoes
exercises and action steps, xix. See also Exercises and action steps

as interaction position, 10–11
perspective shift on, xv–xviii
Networking principles
Appreciate people, 157–180. See also Appreciating people
Avoid formalities and be fun and memorable, 137–156. See also ELF relationships
Being the person they always answer the phone for, 59–86. See also Deepening connections
Being useful, grateful, and valuable, 87–109. See also Gratitude; Utility; Value
Get as close to in-person as you can, 207–228. See also In-person and nearly-in-person communication
Give value on the spot, 181–205. See also Value (on the spot)
How are they suffering and how can I help? xv, xvi, 1–31. See also Mindset for life and relationships
Invest time, attention, money, effort, and energy in relationships, 33–58. See also Investing in relationships
Treat others as they want to be treated, 111–136. See also How to treat people
Norman, André, 202–203
Not Now List, 57–58
Not To Do List, 46–47, 55–56
Nutrition, 47, 124–126

O

100K group, xvii
Ong, Cheri, 93–94
"Opportunity Filter" tool, 95
Overcommitment, 46

P

Pagan, Eben, 67, 68, 74–75, 190
Pain detective mindset, 6–7, 8–10, 12, 19–20
Pain detective mindset exercise, 27–28
Parasites. *See* HALF relationships
Patterson, Kerry, 217
People-picker skills, 72–80, 82, 130–132
Perls, Fritz, 71
Personal ads, 73–77, 86, 148
Phillips, Bill, 166–171
Phone a Friend exercise, 85
Phone caller ID, 62–63. *See also* Deepening connections
Physical suffering, 4
Pickup artistry, 16–18
Pilzer, Paul Zane, 181
Piranha Marketing program, 41
"Pissing me off" exercise, 134–135
Polish, Joe
    addiction and recovery journey of, 13–15, 22–23, 100–101, 229
    appreciation experienced by, 159–162, 166–171
    appreciation practices of, 157–159, 162–163
    background overview, xvii–xviii, 51, 233
    childhood memories, 1–2, 6–7, 62
    Connected: The Joe Polish Story, 233
    connection and disconnection memories, 13–14
    Consumer's Guide to Carpet Cleaning, 24, 91–93
    deepening connection lessons for, 62–63
    high school relationships, 39
    how to treat people lessons for, 111–113, 118–119
    inauthenticity lessons for, 22–23
    in-person connections practices of, 211–212, 219–221
    mission of, xvii, 230–233
    nearly-in-person communication of, 209, 213–214
    as pain detective, 7, 8
    people-picker skill development, 72–77
    personal ad for soulmate by, 76–77
    personal practices for connecting, 104–105
    sabbatical for reassessment and reflection, xix–xx, 229–233
    underappreciation experienced by, 172
    utility practices of, 91–93
    value-on-the-spot experiences of, 181–182, 197–199
    value-on-the-spot practices of, 183–184
Pollock, Jackson, 194
Positive characteristics, 64–65
Positive thinking, 25, 192–193, 200. *See also* Energy
Postcard Challenge exercise, 104, 108
Pre-Suasion (Cialdini), 213
Pulp Fiction (film), 143

R

Rapport-building
    defined, 16
    manners for, 138–140
    in marketing, 24–25
    people-picker skills for, 77–80
    situational awareness and, 122–123
    as skill to be learned, 15–21, 27
    social calibration for, 140–144, 154
    utility in practice for, 94–95
Ratey, John J., 34
Reciprocity, 213, 221–222
Recreational drug "marketing," 194
Relationships. *See* Networking (general); Networking principles

Index

"Respond with ability" (responsibility), 119–120, 125
Return on Genius (Reputation), 42–44, 52–53
Riffing, 147–148, 149–150, 155–156
Ringer, Robert, 165–166
Ringgold, Tim, 89–90
Risky jokes, 141–142
Robbins, Mel, 190
Robbins, Tony, 198
Romantic relationships, 73–77, 86, 116–117, 148
Rotten, Johnny, 112

S

Saying "yes," 46–47
Self-appreciation, 174–176, 178–179
Self-connection
    about, 13–15
    for investing in relationships, 57–58
    rapport and, 15–21
    suffering and, 14
Self-image, 100
Self-worth, 100, 152–153
Sex, 114–115
Sex Pistols, 112
Singles ads, 73–77, 86
Singularity, 164
Situational awareness and behavior
    about, 118–120, 133
    authenticity for, 121–124
    calibration for, 140–144, 154
    for deepening relationships, 64
Sivers, Derek, 47
Sleep, 47
Small talk, 9–10, 216–218
Smith, Babs, 118–119, 141–142
Social calibration, 140–144, 154
Social media deconstruction, 185–188, 200, 202, 231
Socrates, 83
Sonic Recovery (Ringgold), 89
Spending vs. investing mindset, 36–38

Spiritual suffering, 3–4
Stephenson, Sean, 96–97, 105, 126
Strategic Coach, 5, 118–119
Strauss, Neil, 16–18
Strength-and-weakness inventory, 20, 83–85
Suffering
    addiction and, 3–4, 13–14
    connection and disconnection of, 13–15
    as connection tool, 5–6, 26
    defined, 3
    dominoes on, 6, 7, 26
    Genius Network creation for relieving, 28–31
    pain detective mindset for, 6–7, 8–10, 12, 26, 27–28
    suffering point, 11–12, 24–25
    types of, 3
Sullivan, Dan
    on being connected, 95, 105
    on finding the flow, 50
    as Genius Network member, 119
    on overcoming difficulties, 68
    on Polish's humor, 118–119
    on the potential gap, 65
    on selling, 10, 30
    on situational awareness, 119
    social calibration example with, 141–142
    on suffering, 5
Swim with the Sharks without Being Eaten Alive (Mackay), 79, 186, 201–202
Swimmer rescue example, 126

T

Taste and comparison, 124–126
10xTalk podcast, 30, 119
Therapy, 122, 125–126
"Thinking time," 105–106
"This could be a great opportunity for you," 203
Thrive (Huffington), 197
Time, 36–38, 45–47, 50, 54, 56–58
Tiny Habits (Fogg), 146–147

To Do List, 46–47
Tolle, Eckhart, 4
Tone of voice, 209–210
Transactional mindset, xv, xvi,
    9–10, 36–38, 51
Transformative relationships,
    36–38
Trauma bonding, 70–71, 79
Treating others as they want to
    be treated. *See* How to treat
    people
True appreciation, 159–162. *See
    also* Appreciating people
Trust, 15, 18–21, 27
The Truth (Strauss), 16, 17, 28
"Two-minute rule," 184

U

Unappreciated and underappreci-
    ated people, 172–176
Unicorns, 44
Utility (for being connected),
    87–109
    background example, 87–91
    dominoes on, 90, 95, 105,
        106–107
    exercises and action steps,
        108–109
    guide to, 102–105, 107
    in practice, 91–95, 101
    thinking time on, 105–106

V

Validation, 21, 174–176
Value (for being connected),
    87–109
    background example, 87–91
    dominoes on, 90, 101–102,
        105, 106–107
    exercises and action steps,
        108–109
    guide to, 102–105, 107
    other people's languages for,
        117
    in practice, 98–102

thinking time on, 105–106
Value (on the spot), 181–205
    background, 181–182
    dominoes on, 185, 188, 191,
        193, 196, 199–201
    downsides of, 196–199, 201,
        203–204
    exercises and action steps,
        201–205
    for good products, 193–196,
        200–201
    in practice, 183–184
    social media deconstruction
        for, 185–188, 200, 202
    speed of implementation for,
        189–191, 200
    urgency of, 182–185, 200
    "wishful thinking" trap, 191–
        193, 200
Values (personal), 80–82, 155–156
Vicious, Sid, 112
Virgin Records, 112
Virgin Unite, 112–113
Voice, 20–21, 209–210
Voss, Chris, 202–203, 205

W

Walker, Jeff, 143
Weldon, Joel, 139, 227
Wells, Ken, 70–71
"What is hysterical is historical,"
    84
What Needs Solved? exercise, 54
"What's in it for them?" xvi–xvii,
    xx. *See also* Networking
    principles
What's Pissing Me Off? exercise,
    134–135
Winning through Intimidation
    (Ringer), 165–166
"Wishful thinking" trap, 191–193,
    200
Woods, Don, 8
Write Your Appreciation List exer-
    cise, 179–180
Write Your Own Personal Ad exer-
    cise, 86

Y

"Yes," 46–47
"You can't cheat an honest man,"
    127
"Your Purpose in Life" exercise, 85

Z

Zen Buddhism, 4

ACKNOWLEDGMENTS

W riting this book was a long process that started years ago, when I had Reid Tracy, Tucker Max, and Scott Hoffman all come to speak to my Genius Network 100K group. This was the domino that started it all. The writing process was interrupted by a global pandemic and seeing it through was thanks to the efforts of many people.

Thank you to the entire Hay House team, including Reid Tracy, Patty Gift, and my editor, Anne Barthel, who has become more sarcastic and funnier along the way, in spite of her attempts at remaining professional. Thank you to my agent, Scott Hoffman, for coming up with the original title describing what I've been doing for most of my life, and to Dale Carnegie, whose book *How to Win Friends and Influence People* was a major inspiration throughout the process.

Thank you to everyone who helped me with the writing and editing of various drafts of this book in its many stages, including Tucker Max, who worked on the original proposal, and Hal Clifford, who did hours of interviews with me in the very beginning to get an initial draft down on paper.

Thank you to JR for helping create draft two and adding so much more of my life and story into it.

Thank you to Dean Jackson for co-hosting the *I Love Marketing* podcast with me.

Thank you to Anna David, with whom I co-authored a book about addiction recovery in *The Miracle Morning* series with Hal Elrod and for connecting me with Ryan Aliapoulios. It led to a great collaboration that eventually resulted in a final draft and a finished book. I could not have finished it on my own without a boatload of help and hard work—and even as I write this, I'm doing it together with Ryan and Eunice Miller, my amazing assistant of 27 years. Up to the very last paragraph, you both have helped me carry this to the finish line. Hopefully things are easy, lucrative, and fun from here on out!

Thank you to Ben Hardy for your sharp writing and editing skills and for punching things up to make it all even more readable. You are a gem of a human being! Thank you also to the creative team at Gaping Void Culture Design Group for their work on the cover.

Let me again say thank you to Eunice Miller, though it still feels like a complete understatement. I truly cannot put your contributions to my life and business, and to the lives and businesses of so many of our clients over the last 27 years, into words. It would require an entirely new book to document it all. You have helped me at every stage of this process and have been the most instrumental person in my business and life for so long.

Thank you to my current Piranha Marketing and Genius Network team for helping to run the company during my sabbatical and for all the significant work we do day in and day out, including Gina DeLong, Rahkeem Kearney, Chelsea Lucero, Kevin Vanda, Denise McIntyre,

Acknowledgments

Lauren Cortes and Lauren Cannon. Thank you also to Timothy Paulson—we've worked together for 20 years, and even though you say you just retired, I don't believe you! ☺

Thank you to Dan Sullivan and Babs Smith for creating Strategic Coach. I've been a client since 1997 and you have become two of my best friends. Together, we have impacted hundreds of thousands of people, and I can't imagine what the next decade is going to look like.

Thank you to all the people who offered additional input and inspiration (or in some cases permission) through their concepts, stories, and insights (almost all of whom are very close friends and many of whom are best-selling authors themselves), or who otherwise played a major role in the success of this book. Among them are Summer Mulder, Annie Lalla, Harvey Mackay, Gary Chapman, Jennifer Hudye, Dr. Edward Hallowell, Cheri Ong, Michael Fishman and Elaine Glass, Robert B. Cialdini and Bobette Gorden, Steve Sims, Chris Voss, BJ Fogg, Neil Strauss, Ken Wells, and David Bach.

Thank you to everyone who read early versions of the book and who offered endorsements—some are among the names above, but also Victoria Labalme, B. Jeffrey Madoff, Steven Pressfield, Roland Frasier, Paul Johnson, Craig Clemens, Mike Koenigs, Dave Asprey, Jason Fladlien, Verne Harnish, Craig Forte, Tony Rose, Ray Kurzweil, Garrett Gunderson, Laura Catella, Brian Kurtz, Jim Dew, Jim Kwik, Jay Abraham, Steve Ozanich, Greg Ragland, Michael Fishman, Tracy Childers, Lisa Wagner, Guy Daigneault, Cameron Herold, Wesley Kress, Anand Dugar, and Mark Tarbell.

Thanks to the 100K Group and all my Genius Network members. Any problem in the world can be solved with the right Genius Network, and collectively, we've solved thousands of them over the last decade—but there's many more of them ahead for us.

I want to do a shout out to my GeniusX team, including Nick Janicki, Lyle Maxson, Gisele Wyne, and Mike Dudley. Maybe we will eventually put the entire process of this book into VR.

A special thanks to all the people who work with me and have contributed to Genius Recovery and Artists for Addicts, including Akira Chan and Renee Airya, Andre Norman, Mimi Dew, Gabor Maté, Bill Phillips, Jon and Missy Butcher, Leila Parnian, Tony and Mary Miller, Josh Bezoni, Susan Potje, Joe Woodford, Erin Matlock, Nic Peterson, Ken Wells, and Brett Kaufman. Another thank-you to the many inspirational teachers of recovery, including Bill W. and Dr. Bob, Dr. Patrick Carnes, Tommy Rosen, Tim Ringgold, Deanne Adamson, Dr. Dan Engle, Dr. Martin Polanco, Morgan Langan, and Puma St. Angel.

Thanks to all my partners in the 40-acre ghost town we own called Cleator, Arizona—Jason Campbell, Mike Leoni, and Ben Hudye. This is definitely an adventure, and we have our work cut out for us!

To all my friends and authors I haven't already mentioned who have helped make my philosophy of an ELF life and business a reality, including Dr. Ramani Durvasula, Devang Patel, Ken Glickman, Brian Tracy, Robert Ringer, Paul Ross, Craig Ballantyne, Tony Policci, Skyler Allen Parr, Bob Burg, John Sarno, Dr. Daniel Amen, Whitney Jones, Ari Meisel, Dr. Sachin Patel, David Berg, Bob Markowitz, Janet Attwood, Gino Wickman, Alex Mandossian, Les Brown, Keith Cunningham, Brian Kay, Joe Stumpf, Derek Sivers, W. Brett Wilson, Ishan Goel, Martin Howey, Gary Bencivenga, Tim Larkin, Parris

Lampropoulos, Ben Altadonna, Chip Wilson, Brian Scudamore, Patrick Gentempo, Jeff Hays, Robin Robins, Marie Forleo, Wally Wang, Patti Mara, Barbara Hemphill, Jeff Smith, Dan Kennedy, Peter Diamandis, Eben Pagan, Joel Weldon, John Carlton, Terri Lonier, Nick Nanton, Evan Carmichael, JP Sears, Nick Sonnenberg, Alejandra Leibovich, John Raymonds, and Annie Hyman Pratt. There are others I should name—but there are so many it would add another chapter to this book! Please know I appreciate all those I've been impacted by—I hope you know who you are. I will also add additional names to www.WIIFTBook.com/acknowledgments.

I also want to thank all the friends who have been with me on this journey and who I've lost along the way, including Gary Halbert, Dave Kekich, Mark Schneider, Joe Sugarman, Dr. Nathaniel Branden, Dr. Janice Dorn, Dr. Sean Stephenson, and my mom and dad. You've all had such an impact not only on my life, but on the world as well.

A big thank-you to all the givers of the world and a not-so-big thank-you to all the takers—everyone has a purpose in this world, even if it's to temporarily serve as someone else's bad example. I do my best to find the lesson in everything.

Finally, a big thank-you to everyone who has ever been patient and kind to me even when I acted like a jerk to them. We tend to judge ourselves by our intentions and others by their actions, so thanks for doing it the other way around!

I promise to do my best to live up to the words of this book, to help others create ELF lives and businesses, and to keep asking, "What's in it for them?"

ABOUT THE AUTHOR

Joe Polish is the founder of Genius Network, one of the highest-level groups in the world for entrepreneurs. He also curates the Annual Genius Network Event and the 100K Group ($100,000). Genius Network and 100K are home to some of the most successful entrepreneurs alive.

Joe has also helped build thousands of businesses, generated hundreds of millions for his clients, and has been featured in *Inc.*, *Fortune*, *Forbes*, *Success*, and *U.S News & World Report* and on ABC's *20/20*, among others. He has spoken at Stanford University and also hosts three of the top-ranked marketing and business podcasts on iTunes, including *I Love Marketing*, *10xTalk*, and *Genius Network*.

His recent projects include GeniusX, a company he co-founded to bring healing and educational learning programs to VR. He also purchased a 40-acre ghost town with friends called Cleator, Arizona, for an ongoing project that can be followed at www.WhatsYourCleator.com.

His documentary *Connected: The Joe Polish Story* premiered at the historic TCL Chinese Theater in Los Angeles, and his documentary *Black Star* won the Audience Choice Award at the Sedona Film Festival.

Joe's mission with entrepreneurs and Genius Network is "to build a better entrepreneur," and his mission with Genius Recovery is "to change the global conversation about how people view and treat addicts to one of compassion instead of judgment, and to find the most effective forms of treatment and share them with the world."

As an author, Joe has also written five other books, including *Life Gives to the Giver*, which can be downloaded for free at www.JoesFreeBook.com.

Hay House Titles of Related Interest

THE SHIFT, the movie,
starring Dr. Wayne W. Dyer
(available as an online streaming video)
www.hayhouse.com/the-shift-movie

***

*BE YOUR FUTURE SELF NOW: The Science of
Intentional Transformation,* by Dr. Benjamin Hardy

*CHOOSE: The Single Most Important Decision
Before Starting Your Business,* by Ryan Levesque

*OVERDELIVER: Build a Business for a Lifetime Playing the
Long Game in Direct Response Marketing,* by Brian Kurtz

*THE PEOPLE PART: Seven Agreements Entrepreneurs and Leaders
Make to Build Teams, Accelerate Growth, and Banish Burnout
for Good,* by Annie Hyman Pratt

*RISK FORWARD: Embrace the Unknown and
Unlock Your Hidden Genius,* by Victoria Labalme

*WHO NOT HOW: The Formula to Achieve Bigger Goals Through
Accelerating Teamwork,* by Dan Sullivan
with Dr. Benjamin Hardy

*YOUR STAND IS YOUR BRAND: How Deciding "Who to Be" (Not
"What to Do") Will Revolutionize Your Business,*
by Patrick Gentempo

All of the above are available at your local bookstore,
or may be ordered by contacting Hay House (see next page).

***

We hope you enjoyed this Hay House book. If you'd like to receive our online catalog featuring additional information on Hay House books and products, or if you'd like to find out more about the Hay Foundation, please contact:

Hay House, Inc., P.O. Box 5100, Carlsbad, CA 92018-5100
(760) 431-7695 or (800) 654-5126
(760) 431-6948 (fax) or (800) 650-5115 (fax)
www.hayhouse.com® • www.hayfoundation.org

———

Published in Australia by: Hay House Australia Pty. Ltd.,
18/36 Ralph St., Alexandria NSW 2015
Phone: 612-9669-4299 • *Fax:* 612-9669-4144
www.hayhouse.com.au

Published in the United Kingdom by: Hay House UK, Ltd.,
The Sixth Floor, Watson House, 54 Baker Street, London W1U 7BU
Phone: +44 (0)20 3927 7290 • *Fax:* +44 (0)20 3927 7291
www.hayhouse.co.uk

Published in India by: Hay House Publishers India,
Muskaan Complex, Plot No. 3, B-2, Vasant Kunj, New Delhi 110 070
Phone: 91-11-4176-1620 • *Fax:* 91-11-4176-1630
www.hayhouse.co.in

———

Access New Knowledge.
Anytime. Anywhere.

Learn and evolve at your own pace
with the world's leading experts.

www.hayhouseU.com